TO START WITH, FEEL FORTUNATE

TO START WITH, FEEL FORTUNATE

Poetry and Prose by
Peter Meinke
From "Poet's Notebook" Columns in *Creative Loafing*

Illustrations by
Jeanne Clark Meinke

Winner of the
William Meredith Award for Poetry

Poets' Choice

Poets' Choice Publishing

Copyright © 2017 Poets' Choice Publishing
All rights reserved
Printed in the United States of America

Consultant work:
www.WilliamMeredithFoundation.org

Bulk discounts available through www.Poets-Choice.com

Cover image and drawings: Jeanne Meinke
Photo of Author (back cover): Jeanne Meinke
Photo of Author and Artist: Diane Cohen

Library of Congress Cataloging-in-Publication Data pending
ISBN 978-0-9972629-4-0

These essays and images are reprinted with permission from *Creative Loafing*, the original (and continued) publisher of Peter Meinke's "Poet's Notebook" columns. The columns reprinted here appeared from Sept. 6, 2013 to Jan. 5, 2017 in *Creative Loafing*.

Poets' Choice Publishing
337 Kitemaug Road
Uncasville, CT 06382
Poets-Choice.com

This book is dedicated, with love, to our grandparents:

Fred Clark and Ann Philips
Horace Havens and Elizabeth Milner
Harry Meinke and Joannah Twomey
James McDonald and Kathryn Gassert

Immigrants, fishermen, farmers, seamstresses, citizens all, whose ghosts float benevolently through and above these essays and drawings.

ACKNOWLEDGMENTS

I want to thank everyone quoted in these columns, especially the poets, for the privilege of using parts of their poems. These Notebooks, literally and figuratively, begin and end with them.

Many thanks as well to *Creative Loafing* for offering a place for these meditations and drawings to feel at home, and to David Warner and Scott Harrell for their faithful and meticulous editing and help all along the line.

I especially want to thank Ed Ochester and the University of Pittsburgh Press for allowing me to quote so amply from books of mine that they have published.

Finally, Richard Harteis, President of the William Meredith Foundation, and Barbara Shaw, editor extraordinaire, can't be thanked enough for their work on this book; nor can Jeanne, my wife for sixty years, for her brilliant drawings. She likes to point out that we "collaborate in separate rooms."

PUBLISHER'S ACKNOWLEDGMENT

The publication of *To Start With, Feel Fortunate* is made possible largely through a contribution by Fred Van Aken in memory of his wife Anna. She was a talented artist and teacher and one of the sweetest people you would ever want to meet in life. We are fortunate to have had her with us for a while, and for Fred's friendship to the foundation. Peter's wife, Jeanne Clark Meinke has provided the charming sketch of Anna in the style of other fine drawings in the book.

Additional funding has been provided by Bill and Rosalie Deitz, as well as William Meredith Foundation Treasurer, Nancy Frankel.

ANNA VAN AKEN

CONTENTS

Preface • xi
The American Living Room: A Tract • xv

2013

Booboisie • 3
Light Rail • 7
Names • 11
Seamus Heaney • 15
Do or Die • 19
Mazzaroli's Cannon • 23
Toss Me a Meatball • 27
ACA:Fix It • 31
3 Christmas Limericks • 35

2014

Early Words • 41
Year of the Woman • 45
Unhealthy Activities • 49
Saving a Generation • 53
Japanese Bourbon • 57
Putin Rides the Wave • 61
Backward and Forward: John Donne • 65
A Kinder Pope • 69
Wipeout • 73
Mayday • 77
Happy Fathers • 81
Unsmiling • 85
Stuck with Traffic • 89
Poetry & Music • 93
Accidental Lives • 97
On Foreign Shores • 101
Poetry & Age • 105
Poets & Scientists Unite • 109
Feminism & Language • 113

Flip-flops • 117
The Good Doctor • 121
ISIS Crisis • 125
Walking the Walk • 129
Confidence • 133
Carousel Christmas • 137

2015
Polish Lessons • 143
Hawaiian Sigh • 147
Racism & Kramer • 151
Ready for Hillary? • 155
The Liberal Arts • 159
Oil on the Fire • 163
Bus Story • 167
Sweet Briar • 171
Word Stars • 175
Our Lady of the Cherries • 179
Healthy Choice • 183
Winter Revisited • 187
Laureate • 191
Two Households • 195
Wand'ring Minstrels • 199
Nuclear Deal • 203
Christie in Wonderland • 207
Root Causes • 211
Odd Jobs • 215
Whiz, Bang! The Nuclear Accord • 219
Taxi! • 223
Bernie Sanders • 227
A Tale of Two Popes • 231
Elf-Employment • 235
Poetry & Broccoli • 239
The Sign of The Dove • 243

CONTENTS

2016

We'll Always Have Paris • 249
Trump • 253
All the World's a Stage • 257
Maureen Vanderbilt • 261
Stampeding Elephants • 265
Luck of the Irish • 269
Assuming the Position • 273
Ybor City • 277
Drinking Cooperation • 281
The Bibliophiles • 285
Baseball: The Fan Problem • 289
The Cost of War • 293
William Butler Yeats • 297
Mass Murder, Again • 301
A Friend in Cheeses • 305
Greatness • 309
Education • 313
Post Master • 317
Evolutionary Politics • 321
Poet Edward Field • 325
Suicide • 329
Loose Notes • 333
Old Age • 337
Trump Wins! • 341
Changes • 345
Pulse: the Brillantina Project • 349
The Dying Kimball • 353

2017

Ringing in the New • 359

About the Author and Artist • 363

PREFACE

By Richard Harteis

The original subtitle to this book read, "80+ Poet's Notebook' Columns from *Creative Loafing*," a journal from St. Petersburg, Florida written by the current Poet Laureate of Florida, Peter Meinke. In an earlier book, *Truth and Affection,* similar essays give Meinke's take on American culture in a voice that has been described as sensitive, compassionate, witty and wise. Since that book, Meinke has continued to write his astute observations about American life and how poetry can guide us toward a more spiritual and fuller life. As David Warner, the Editor of that previous book writes in the introduction, "'Poet's Notebook' is difficult to define, a tasty bouillabaisse of poetry, politics, and personal essay…winning hearts and minds of all ages for six years now and a few awards along the way." And later, "He [Meinke] is always more self-effacing than self-righteous—warning that the urge to settle on a single answer is inevitably dangerous. He is suspicious of absolutism of all kinds, happy to skewer the divisive rhetoric of Tea Party mythologies and scientists' quest for a Theory of Everything. He's more a fan of Chaos Theory himself…."

To Begin With, Feel Fortunate was written in part in the chaotic year running up to the election of the new president and is a passionate analysis of how we got to where we are as a nation, and what may be in store for us. As Peter has said in an interview, "You have to remember that even the poets who live in garrets are citizens, and I urge them to use their voices and partake in the actual goings-on of our country." Like William Meredith, who was a good friend in the old days, Meinke's work is not written from the ivory tower. Like Meredith, he feels writers and intellectuals have an obligation to speak the truth and shame the devil. And if poetry and prose are to be useful in our lives, they must first of all be honest or otherwise risk being merely window dressing in a fancy American living room.

Critics have argued that poetry fails to the exact extent it attempts to be didactic. And though he is a teacher and has lived to see much change in this country, Meinke's work does not attempt to preach. It's the voice of a really nice guy you'd like to have a beer with at the local pub to hash out whatever you have on your mind: the world series, the future of the stock market, the state of the union. He would never consider his fellow citizens "deplorable" and admires the hard-working, middle-class as well as poets who celebrate their life, like Philip Levine and yes, Bob Dylan.

Regardless of the point Meinke wishes to make, poetry is always the touchstone, the starting point of his reflections: common sense enhanced with rhyme, rhythm, metaphor and philosophy that goes beyond mere rhetorical flair. Reading these essays, one thinks of Will Rogers, Mark Twain, or even an upscale Garrison Keillor. He challenges and delights a reader with accurate, elegant, and important observations. One may not always agree with the positions he takes, or the poets he quotes, but it's hard to resist or deny the honesty and clarity of his vision.

In the ten years since William Meredith's death, the Meredith Foundation board has chosen a wide variety of poets to receive this award in terms of style, reputation, gender, and politics. They range from the beautiful, Baudelaire-like poems reflecting the fractured and kaleidoscopic shape of David Fisher's mind to the exquisite reflections on the Gulf coast inhabitants after hurricane Katrina by US Poet Laureate, Natasha Trethewey, to Bulgaria's national poet and master lyricist, Lyubomir Levchev. This year's award brings home the recognition of an American poet writing at the top of his powers.

As a foundation we cannot endorse a particular political party, can-

PREFACE

didate or policy. But we can celebrate considered, compassionate, and honest thinking when a poet asserts his First Amendment rights. Such poetry and prose can be a bridge between camps in our divided culture. As teacher and counselor Therese Tappouni has said of Peter Meinke, "He is the soul of reason, though his feelings run deep. His willingness to listen to others is rare. My New Year's wish is that others like Peter will rise up and demand a return to humane discourse among the citizens of this country, and a backing off from the 'us vs. them' that defines us."

A final word must be said about the drawings which illustrate these essays by Peter's accomplished artist wife, Jeanne Clark Meinke. Her drawings have graced the pages of *The New Yorker* more than a hundred times over the years, for example, and many other major publications. Her sketch of William Meredith was done after his stroke and forms the center of the medallion for this award on the cover. How beautifully she captures the questioning glance and gentle eyes of the poet and even his uneven smile with simple lines. It is a look which seems to ask, "What are you thinking, do you love the fair world?" We have included it again in conjunction with Meredith's poem, "The American Living Room – A tract" from which the title of this book is taken.

Aside from several collaborations with Peter, Jeanne Meinke's sketches have been featured in their own right in works such as *Lines from Wildwood Lane* published by the University of Tampa Press. In the words of Eckerd College President Donald Eastman, she is "a nationally renowned master of the line drawing, a visual Emily Dickinson." Her pen and ink drawings are as accurate and crystal clear as Peter's prose and enhance his work with truth and affection too.

How lucky we are as a culture to have these gregarious, loving, intelligent, and humane artists among us to help show us the way, to challenge and delight—American intelligence at its best. Long may they thrive and prosper as we enter an uncertain future which will require wise men and women who believe that the world can and needs to be a better place. As Meredith has written in the hopeful last lines of his short, signatory poem, A Major Work:

> "whether from brute need
> Or divine energy
> At last mind, eye, and ear
> And the great sloth heart will move."

The American Living Room: A Tract

I
Ideally, you should be in your own
when you read this. Think of it as an oddity—
the one indoor space where living
is deliberately pursued, as in others
we transact dining, sleeping, bathing,
perhaps TV or children. Wherever there are two,
one should be kitchen. For the rich,
rooms can be spun out indefinitely:
drawing-, dressing-, morning-, and special
chambers called library, pantry, nursery.
Many still house their cars.

II
Most people inhabit shelters too small
to partition off with words, and always
some people have none. Is it better
to feel at fault for this, or not
to feel at fault? The meagerest American house
is a gross Hilton compared to where most people
take shelter on the inclement world.
To start with, feel fortunate.

III
You have made the effort to dress yourself
in character, probably well beyond the requirement
of mere covering—you have already risked
that much misunderstanding. Then comes
this second habiliment, no matter how
reluctant or minimal a statement,
a room which gives you away: with the things
you've acquired at cost, the things you've been given

and kept, the things you choose to exhibit.
The accumulation seems to have been only partly voluntary.
Yet no one you'd want to know could stay
for a month, in a rented room in Asia, without
this telltale silt beginning to settle.
When people die, their children have to come dig
for them like Winckelmanns, among many false Troys.

    IV
Prisons recognize the need to arrest
this form of identity. Cells
are deliberately ill-fitted uniforms
which you are issued to wear over
the deliberately ill-fitted cloth ones. You
are put there to forgo living.
Military quarters may appear more permissive,
yet the space for personal effects is limited
and subject to unscheduled inspection. Nobody
is encouraged to bring along a two-volume dictionary,
a Hopi mask, a valuable paperweight, to a war
or to the interminable rehearsals of camp and shipboard.

    V
The room we're in now is like something you've said,
whether offhand or considered. It's in a dialect
that marks you for a twentieth-century person
(enthusiastic about this? dragging your feet?),
rich or poor or—more commonly—a little of both;
belonging to a nation and an eclectic culture.
The room risks absurdity, as you risked that again
when you put your clothes on this morning,
but because it is capable of being judged
apart from you, in your absence, the risk is greater.
Why has he got and kept this, and only this?

anyone can ask. Why so much? To others
this room is what your scent is to a dog.
You can't know it or help it.

    VI
With us in America, a person who has a printed poem
is likely to have a living room (though not always—
there will always be some to whom poetry is not an amenity).
For reasons of its own, poetry has come to this,
with us. It has somehow gone along
with the privileges of the nation
it intends to change, to dispossess of material demons.
Admittedly, this is part of its present difficulty.
For the moment, though, you are holding this poem.
Its aim is that of any artifact: to ingratiate.
It would like nothing better
than to be added to the dear clutter here.

JEANNE

2013

H. L. MENCKEN

SEPTEMBER 3, 2013

Booboisie

Bold with adrenaline, mindless, shaking,
God damn it, no! I rasp at him behind me,
Wrenching the leather from his grasp. It
breaks like a wishbone.

For a long time, America's been playing Variations on a Theme, and the theme is Race. There's been progress, *e.g.*, President Barack Obama—but the Republican Party, with help from the Supreme Court, is working tirelessly to restrict voting laws so this can't happen again. And pretty much since 1861 the same states, instead of saying 'OK, you win,' still would prefer to secede. The new movie, "The Butler" gives a stirring summary of this spotted progress, and should be required viewing by all the high schools in the country. Hey, it has Oprah in a starring role; what's not to like?

On October 3, 1995, we were at a bar in the Newark, New Jersey, terminal, waiting for a flight home. The usual airport buzz filled the place, until someone yelled for QUIET! A TV newsman was about to announce the jury's verdict in the double-murder trial of Orenthal James Simpson. What followed was the opposite of the Trayvon Martin reaction: the blacks in the bar stood up and roared their approval of "Not Guilty," and the whites sat quietly, as if shell-shocked.

Whatever one thinks of either verdict, it's clear we have two countries out there, reminiscent of Rudyard Kipling's dark prophecy about East and West—'Never the twain shall meet.' Kipling was a conservative pessimist, and the real world, repeatedly shooting itself in the foot (and elsewhere), keeps trying to prove him right. One large branch of these countries was given a name some time ago.

The great editor and curmudgeon H. L. Mencken coined the word 'booboisie' to refer to a section of America's middle class that, far from fading away, has actually grown more powerful. His booboisie were *gullible, anti-science,* and *angry* (sound familiar?), believing in the 1920's equivalent of Fox News, Creationism, and Separation of the Races. The high point of Mencken's journalistic career was the so-called Monkey Trial where, in 1925, a Tennessee high school teacher was tried for teaching about evolution. The legendary lawyer Clarence Darrow debated three-time Democratic presidential candidate William Jennings Bryan about evolution and the Bible, with Mencken covering the trial for *The Baltimore Sun*.

In *Inherit the Wind*, the famous movie about the event, Spencer Tracy plays Darrow, Fredric March plays Bryan, and Gene Kelly plays Mencken (to Mencken's great benefit, at least in the looks and charm departments). Mencken would have had a field day covering the Martin/Zimmerman trial, beginning with the choosing of the jury: six Southern women—not a single one of them black—who claimed to have no opinion about the shooting.

A more polite word for booboisie would be 'Philistines,' used by the poet Mathew Arnold (1822-1888) to mean, more or less, the "unenlightened," antagonistic to progress. You can trace it back to the Bible—a bit unfairly—where the Philistines (the enemies of the Hebrews) were the ones that Samson slew with the jawbone of an ass. We have lots of those jawbones still, but seem to be a bit short of Samsons.

Bryan, who stood for many of the ideas, included Prohibition which Mencken detested, died in his sleep five days after the trial, confident of victory, in certain knowledge of where he was going. He did win, of course, the state being Tennessee, though the teacher was fined only $100.

Not all the booboisie's ideas were bad. In 1931, after Mencken referred to Arkansas as "the apex of moronia," the Arkansas Legislature passed a motion to pray for his soul. I would have voted for that, even though Mencken once declared that "a poet more than thirty years old is simply an overgrown child." Well, that's possible. Next Thursday, September 12th, is his birthday. *Requiescat in pace*, wherever he is.

Only now turning, I see a tall boy running,
fifteen, sixteen, dressed thinly for the weather.
Reaching the streetlight he turns a brown face briefly
phrased like a question.

–both quotes from "Effort at Speech" by William Meredith (1919-2007)

ST. PETE TRAIN STATION

SEPTEMBER 9, 2013

Light Rail

The best thing about Tampa Bay is our light rail system. Built mostly with government money, it has almost singlehandedly 1) kept the Rays from leaving St. Pete by dropping off fans from near and far close to the gates, like almost all major league parks; 2) cut down on the horrific traffic between the cities at rush hour; 3) extended our life spans by easing the stress of trips to the airport; 4) helped keep our air clean by lessening our dependence on oil, 5) solved our downtown parking problem, and 6) gave us safer, cheaper, more dependable and aesthetically pleasing transportation.

...O, sorry, that's right, Governor Scott and the Republican legislature turned the rail proposition down—*Nothing to make President Obama look good!*—despite our voting for it, and all the jobs it would have created. If we're voting, this decision alone makes Scott our Worst Governor.

Living in Amherst, MA, for one summer, Jeanne and I were pleased to learn that Emily Dickinson's father, Edward—unlike Governor Scott—was the driving force in bringing that new invention, the railroad, to the little town of Amherst in 1853; now part of Amtrak, it connects Amherst to all the major cities surrounding it. Dickinson Street and Railroad Street run parallel to each other, running into College Street, where we lived that summer, so it was easy to imagine Emily listening to the trains, and writing, as one chugged by...

> *...Around a Pile of Mountains —*
> *And supercilious peer*
> *In Shanties — by the sides of Roads —*
> *And then a Quarry pare...*

Once upon a time, before being undone by mismanagement, buses, and Big Oil, a railroad/trolley combination in St. Petersburg, with a charming Victorian station along our own Railroad Avenue, led directly to the Wharf, which became the Pier, which is about to become...well, who knows? You could go all over St. Pete by trolley, 15 rides for $1.00! Years ago, one of our boys found a heavy iron spike buried in our back yard, which borders on 24th Avenue South. The boys were used to finding clusters of shells from an old Spanish fort that once was built below here—but what was this spike from? Some old-timers in our neighborhood (we arrived in 1966) told us it was from the old trolley line—the last one torn up in 1949—which used to end right behind our house.

When we lived in Neuchâtel, Switzerland (population c. 35,000), the trolley was right below our house (we had to cross the tracks to get to the lake). We could take the trolley downtown, the bus to the University, or the train to Geneva, Paris, Heidelberg, Rome, anywhere in Europe. The city's perched on the slope of the Jura Mountains, so the train station is above, with a view of Neuchâtel's rooftops, the lake below, and the Alps on the other side of the lake. It's a charming but steep walk down, and the children loved it. If we had luggage we took the trolley. Buses rolled through for the surrounding villages. What you *don't* need is a car.

The year we lived there, Henry Genz, a distinguished Eckerd college French professor (Neuchâtel is French-speaking) stopped by for a surprise visit, but we were out of town. He left a note saying he was sorry he missed us, but had enjoyed the best trout he'd ever eaten in the train station's café. This was no accident: across Europe and in parts of America, you'll find some of the best restaurants in or right by the train stations.

Light rail and trolleys make a city better, and the Worst Thing about Tampa Bay is we don't have it. By the time our leaders get around to building it, it will take three times longer and cost ten times more (we seem to be working on a similar strategy with our Pier). Tampa Bay's a great area, but Emily Dickinson would feel sorry for us: We can't watch an iron horse galloping through the neighborhoods—

> *Neighing like Boanerges –*
> *Then – punctual as a Star*
> *Stop – docile and omnipotent*
> *At its own stable door –*

> –quotes from #585 in *The Complete Poems of Emily Dickinson* (Little, Brown & Co.)

CANDELABRA

OCTOBER 3, 2013

Names

*..... I know the song
of names by now   seductive and misleading:
Cherry Birch   Blue Birch   Black Birch   Sweet
and the High Himalayan   though it's hard as hell
to say just which is which ...*

    A century ago, seeing my students' resentful eyes because I was keeping them inside on a fine sun-filled day, the old cliché would come to mind, "Hey, pay attention—I've forgotten more than you'll ever know." But now, facing students only occasionally, a less comfortable thought rises as I pause, a bit confused, in mid-sentence: "I really *have* forgotten it."

    At dinner a while back, Jeanne said she'd read a good review of a TV show about, um, the piano player. "Piano player?" I said.

    "You know, the one with the candelabra ..." Well, OK, no problem.

    Later, after that show, we turned the channel to "Network," a 1976 movie we'd missed somehow, and right away an actress sashayed onto the scene with a sultry and familiar walk.

    Who's that?

    "She was in 'Chinatown,'" Jeanne offered. *But what's her name?* After a while, I said, "She was in 'Barfly,' too—that movie about the poet whatshisname."

    Later on—as usual—we remembered: Faye Dunaway and Charles Bukowski. But as we were dozing off Jeanne wondered why names in particular are so hard to recall, much harder than places and objects (like candelabra).

"Every Tom, Dick, and whozit forgets names," I said. But maybe that's not true, and only seems that way because our friends tend to be tipsy septuagenerians. The basic problem is that names don't have meaning in the usual sense. Our brains are programmed to remember by association, but names are pretty randomly assigned, and even ones that have or suggest meaning (Peter Singer or Ginger Baker, for example) are usually misleading. And a lot of names today are not only hard to remember, but hard to pronounce. The Rays' Yunel Escobar had three hits yesterday.

We occasionally try to do something about our memory slide. Staying for a while in the Catskills, I decided to study its flora and fauna. I was doing fine until I started on the birch trees, many varieties of which were scattered around the property. The more I looked up their names the more confused I got—'Knowledge splits its subjects into chunks' is another line from today's poem—and soon gave up.

Jeanne, having more staying power, took a do-it-yourself course on remembering names, called Mega-Memory. Working on her computer, she got to the point where she could recognize whole groups of faces, using associative methods (Alison / a lice; Bailey / bay leaf, etc.). We were both proud of her ability, and she'd show it off on occasion. But it took practice and too much time, and gradually she got bored with doing it—"I don't want this to be my life," she said. She had her Poet's Notebook drawings to do.

Recently we sat down with a large group of people, and—almost inevitably in such a mix—the difficulty of names came up, so Jeanne told her Mega-story, concluding that indeed, she *had* learned to remember names for a while, but now, she said, "I'm just like the rest of you."

"Whoever you are," I added, unhelpfully.

We've decided to live with this handicap, somewhat mollified by discovering it's a wide-spread affliction, not entirely concentrated on our age group.

Just last night, we were talking about one of our *bêtes noires*, the bugaboo who got all the Republicans to pledge never to raise taxes. Of course, we forgot his name. Jeanne thought that it began with an 'N.' "I'd like to name a doll after him and stick pins in it."

"Good," I said. "If we remember it, let's get the spelling right."

As Jimmy Durante might have said, at the end of one of his shows, "Goodnight Mrs. . . um, wherever you are." Began with a "C."

> *. . . And on that big one*
> *warbling his dumb head off sits a goldfinch—*
> *some kind of goldfinch . . .*
>
> –both quotes from 'The Student' in *Night Watch on the Chesapeake* by Peter Meinke, U. of Pittsburgh Press 1987

SEAMUS HEANEY

OCTOBER 17, 2013

Seamus Heaney

Between my finger and my thumb
The squat pen rests; snug as a gun.

   –from "Digging" by Seamus Heaney (1939-2013)

One evening when Seamus Heaney had given a poetry reading in Dublin, and attended the fine party afterwards, he was speeding through the Irish countryside, wanting to get home and having had a wee bit too much to drink. Soon, a white car with the familiar roof-light and siren showed up behind him, so he pulled over and waited for the policeman, who gruffly asked to see his license. After reading the small print, the officer peered at Heaney closely. "Heaney," he said. "Do you be the poet?"

"I am, sir," pronounced Heaney, with dignity.

The officer straightened up. "Pass, brother," he said, and waved him on.

That sounds true. The history of Ireland may be mad and violent, but it has always loved its writers. In a short walk through Dublin, where Heaney lived most of his life—dying there on August 30th— you can't go far before bumping into a statue of Oliver Goldsmith, George Bernard Shaw, Oscar Wilde, or even some fictional characters, like Anna Livia Plurabelle, from James Joyce's *Finnegan's Wake*. Submerged in water, Anna, popularly called "the Floozy in the Jacuzzi," is the spirit of the River Liffey, which runs saucily through Dublin. (The statue of Joyce with his walking cane is known as "The

Prick with a Stick": fame in Ireland, like the language itself, is a two-edged sword.) I can only imagine what they'll call Heaney (unfortunately pronounced HEEny) when they get around to *his* statue.

We were last in Dublin on a cold November day, and it took a lot of coins and kicking to get the little heater in our b&b to work, after which we headed out along the Liffey to the Writer's Museum, to read about Nobel Laureate Heaney and a multitude of others. Beautifully displayed in a handsome Georgian mansion on Parnell Square, the Museum's a treasure chest of quirky information about its writers. Who would have guessed that in their youth Oscar Wilde (boxing) and Samuel Beckett (cricket) were outstanding athletes?

Dublin's called a City of Writers, which made me think of Tampa and St. Petersburg, where there's already an organization called City of Writers, founded in 2009 to increase the support and profile of *our* inkslingers. We've more poets right here in Tampa Bay who've reached out beyond our borders than you might think. The proper response to poetry is more poetry, so here, with apologies for many omissions—no space, no time!—I've made a little list of our poets, in the spirit of the great Irish poet we'll miss and admire, Seamus Heaney

Tampa Bay Poets

Hawkins Hopler Wallace Ward
Dawson Sellers Martinez Byrd
Not too hard to buy a bard
a beer on Kennedy Boulevard
dreaming of the perfect word

Everyone here can bang the gong:
Riegel and Sukrungruang
Shomer Tokley Russo Wilt
A reputation's being built
Mathews Morrill Curbelo Carroll

sip from the Muse's sherry barrel
Though Tampa Bay's not Dublin yet
the pubs are open appetites whet
the writers write we're all in debt
writing together from Bay to Sea:

Here's to Seamus and Poetry!

   –by Peter Meinke, sure and whose sainted mother was
    Kathleen McDonald

NEWT GINGRICH

OCTOBER 31, 2013

Do or Die

Half a fake, half a fib,
Half a fraud onward,
All in the Valley of Lies
Charged the two hundred
"Forward the Lie Brigade!
Tread on the poor!" he said
Into the Valley of Lies
Rode the two hundred . . .

The 230 Republicans didn't charge madly forward like a tribe of eager colonialists dumping tea, but surged together in organized ranks with their suicidal attack on "Obamacare," reminiscent of another famous battle a century after the original Tea Party in Boston.

On October 25th, 1854, in what has been called "the stupidest exploit in British military history," the British light cavalry, armed only with sabers, galloped into the cannons and rifles of the waiting Russian army at Balaclava, during the Crimean War. The soldiers, ordered by the now infamous Lord Raglan (though there remains some debate on who gave the order), charged bravely forward—*Theirs not to reason why, / Theirs but to do and die*—and their useless and bloody defeat is mainly remembered now because of Tennyson's resounding poem, "The Charge of the Light Brigade," written shortly after the bloody slaughter disguised as a battle.

The leader behind today's Tea Party's charge is usually said to be Senator Ted Cruz, the militant Canadian who prospered as his troops got decimated. During the skirmish that shut down the government, Cruz talked without stopping in both the foreground and background, whipping Republicans into a religious fervor till they were all talking in tongues. So many words poured out that the original simple idea kept getting buried: the Tea Party wanted to destroy "Obamacare," despite it being the law of the land. It's like a gang of prudes threatening to close down the Metropolitan Museum of Art unless it gets rid of Renoir's "The Bathers" because they don't approve of those bare bosoms.

But the intellectual power behind this movement isn't Cruz, whom even many Republicans call frankly wacko; it's Newt Gingrich, the Commander-in-Chief of the take-no-prisoners policy of politics, adapted with evangelical enthusiasm by 40 House members of the Tea Party, who in turn acted as Sergeants in the ranks, enforcing discipline. In the 1980's Gingrich surged forward as a pompous imitation of Gilbert and Sullivan's character, the "Very model of a Modern Major-general" (who "knows the Kings of England and can quote the Fights historical"). Applying cutthroat capitalism to politics, he preached that compromise is the enemy of success: the idea is to crush and devour the opponent, to block *everything* he or she tries to do.

After his initial victories, Gingrich was brought up on ethics charges, and flamboyantly imploded—but his "downfall" came too late. The Republican Party had been impregnated, and Rosemary's baby was hatching.

The election of a black liberal Democrat as President in 2008 was a galvanizing spark, igniting both conscious and unacknowledged passions in Western and Southern Republicans, still unhappy about the Civil Rights Bill. Now the bulk of those state have switched from resisting Civil Rights to gerrymandering and suppressing the Vote. Race warfare has broadened into class warfare against the lazy, lawless, and uninsured poor.

Republican bumper-stickers shout "100% anti-Obama!" It's a headlong charge that in the long run they can't win, but in the battle they're bringing down a lot of innocent people with them. This tactic will rise again in a month or two. Their constituents, most of them hypocritically dependent on the government, look on them as brave soldiers. They may be brave, but they're fighting the wrong battle with the wrong leaders in an old war.

When will their anger fade?
O the wild lies they made!
All the world wonder'd.
Laugh at the Lie Brigade,
Weep at the harm they did,
Shameless two hundred.

–from "The Charge of the Lie Brigade"
with apologies to Alfred, Lord Tennyson

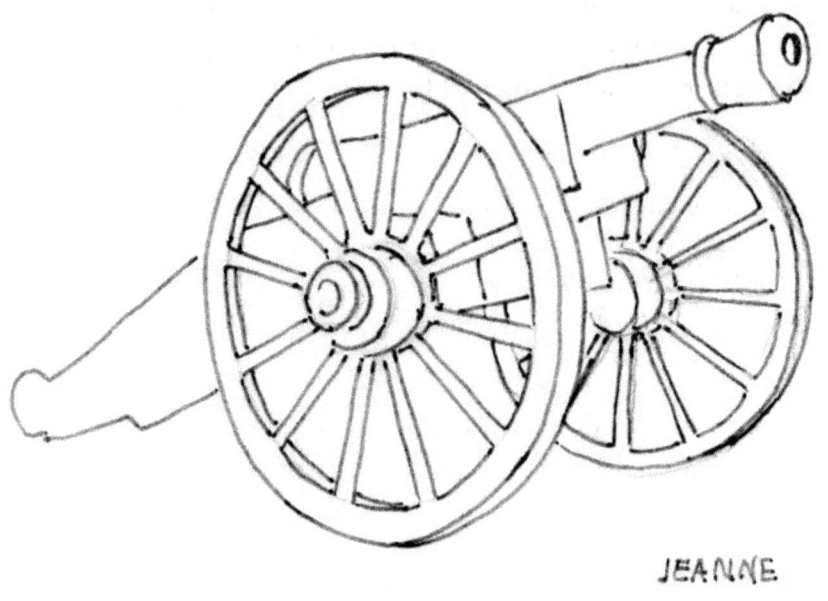

MAZZAROLI'S CANNON

NOVEMBER 14, 2013

Mazzaroli's Cannon

Gods cluster like orgiastic barnacles
along the barrel of this exquisite machine

heating up as shots explode toward flesh
or fortress   death aesthetically pleasing

ah, the elegant weapons! . . .

In the fall semester of 1992, Jeanne and I were living in the basement of the Eckerd College Student Center—a five-story Georgian rowhouse on Gower Street in London. The water pipes from upstairs ran behind the headboard of our bed, and we'd wake with dreams of being water-boarded, until we forbade showers after 10 p.m.

When we came up from the basement for air, we'd take our students to visit various museums, and one of our favorites was the Wallace Collection, in an historic mansion on Manchester Square. We're particularly fond of small museums that leave us excited instead of exhausted; and the Wallace is one of the best (admission free, open seven days a week—come on, America!)

The Collection specializes in 17th and 18^h Century paintings—*e.g.*, Nicholas Poussin's "A Dance to the Music of Time" (1634) and Franz Hal's "The Laughing Cavalier" (1624)—but to my mind (childlike, corrupt and male), its real attraction is its "Arms and Armour" collection. In stately rooms, thousands of weapons are displayed for their beauty and elegance: cannons, rifles, pistols, shields, helmets, daggers, swords, scimitars, sabers, axes, pikes, lances, arrows, bayonets—there are more English names for pointy things that kill you than Eskimo words for snowflakes.

I admit to conflicting emotions as I look at these gorgeous objects. Although I served in the Army as a post-Korea draftee, I have at least semi-pacifist leanings. I feel in general that—even leaving out the "innocent" victims—soldiers are sent to kill exactly those kinds of men they would really like in peacetime, ordered to do so by exactly the kinds of men they don't like.

Our son Pete once told a pacifist friend of ours, as Pete was considering letting his name be pulled out of a hat for Vietnam, "I don't think I can call myself a pacifist when I feel like shooting the bastard who wants to draft me."

I wonder how Wayne LaPierre, the NRA marksman, I mean spokesman, would feel about the Wallace collection. I don't think he'd enjoy it: his view of weapons is universally utilitarian, having said "The only way to stop a bad man with a gun is with a good man, woman or child with a gun." Or something like that.

It's unlikely that the Wallace arsenal ever stopped anybody, except visitors who walk by the glassed-in exhibits. The weapons, like Mazzaroli's cannon, could probably have been used, but the head curator, Jeremy Warren, assured me that these were primarily "parade weapons," made for show. Rulers and other rich men would roll them out, or wear them, for parades and formal ceremonies; or to be formally painted grasping them with phallic complacency.

In her drawing for this column, Jeanne has stripped the cannon back to its original and functional shape, which Mazzaroli's intricate decorations tend to hide, or at least distract the viewer from seeing that this is a weapon. Though it makes my head spin to think about, I believe that this art—like almost all art—is amoral, but not immoral. (To me, the NRA's support of AK-47's, etc., for civilian use is immoral.)

Jeanne isn't alone in not liking the violence of football, but maybe decorative weapons are to war what football is to violence: a way of moving it off the streets over to the aesthetic sphere, trying to frame and contain our natural destructive tendencies.

But even as I think this, in the week of Armistice Day, somewhere in the back of my head I can hear old Tom Lehrer (born 1928, and still around) laughing at us, while he sings again the scientist's *apologia*: 'Vunce the rockets are up who cares vere they come down? / Dot's not my department!' says Werner von Braun."

>   *. . . so when*
>   *the inevitable bad ending ends he*
>
>   *and all artists shall be ready*
>   *with their stunning ivory-crusted*
>   *gold-leaf and silvered caskets*
>
>   –both quotes from 'Mazzaroli's Cannon' by Peter Meinke, in *Scars* (1996), U. of Pittsburgh Press.

WEBER'S GRILL

NOVEMBER 28, 2013

Toss Me a Meatball

Now Adam knew Eve his wife, and she conceived and bore Cain, saying, "I have gotten a man with the help of the Lord."

–Genesis 4:1

Scrabbling around in our garage this week, I came across our old grill, and thought—a bit ruefully—that I've not only given up smoking, I've given up smoking turkeys. What next, grilled cheese? This is a vegetarian house but the rules are fluid.

On Thanksgiving, I used to get up at 5 a.m., dust off the grill, fill the pan with water, add some mesquite chips to the charcoal, heave the turkey on the grill, and try to squirt the lighter fluid and light the coals in the right order. Jeanne would have made some tasty marinade with which I'd baste the massive bird throughout the morning, watching it slowly turn that delectable brown color as the scent of roasting turkey spread around the neighborhood. The thought occurs to me that these turkeys aren't vegetarians. They don't get those Butterball breasts from veggies.

Often when it was done I'd carry the bird proudly out to the park in front of our house, setting it on a table filled with other gifts for the neighborhood's Thanksgiving banquet, featuring smoked fish, Virginia-cured ham, heaps of sweet potatoes, cranberries, and pumpkin and mince pies for the hungry pilgrims of Driftwood . . .

Jeanne became a vegetarian about 20 years ago. She had an ambiguous health scare, and wasn't about to wait around to see what would happen: she read a lot of books and, despite being famous for her chicken Vindaloo, decided vegetarianism was the way to go. This seems to have been a wise choice, as at the advanced age of X, she's one healthy whipper-snapper.

I too am healthier as, not counting an occasional squirrel, no meat can enter our doors. Jeanne looks on this as win/win, as she often lets me talk her into going out to dinner, where she enjoys her Caesar salad with salmon, while tossing meatballs to me like fish to a gaping pelican at the Pier (now also closed, come to think of it).

It's difficult to debate a vegetarian. Jeanne and many other 'near-vegetarians' eat fish, particularly salmon, for their health, which seems a tad contradictory—but "I won't eat anything that screams when you kill it" is pretty tough to argue with. The idea of my chicken sandwich shrieking like Maria Sharapova makes me hesitate. Injection with poison would make chickens inedible, and electric chairs would be expensive. Besides, vegetarianism seems good for our environment, in a way that cattle ranches and chicken coops aren't, so pointing out a few philosophical inconsistencies doesn't cut much tasty cheese.

Like many of my Tea Party friends, when cornered I often turn to the Bible, but this, too, poses problems on the subject. Cain, as we know, was Adam and Eve's first-born, followed closely by Abel, both brought safely into the world without Obamacare. Cain was "a tiller of the ground," and Abel, not wanting to copy his brother, raised sheep. Violence then entered the world—*via* males: that seems right—when Cain beat Abel to death because God accepted Abel's offering of roast lamb but turned down Cain's vegetarian medley.

One would naturally think that Cain, the vegetarian, was right, being the first born and so, we've been taught by psychologists, an over-achiever. But why did God turn his vegetables down? From the very Beginning, it seems to have been a case of *De gustibus non est disputandum.*

I've therefore decided to follow the Greeks, who are much clearer, though not as interesting, on the subject. Their general advice—summed up by Aristotle—was to follow the "golden mean," moderation in all things, guided by wisdom and experience. You can see why the overheated Tea Party prefers the Bible to Plato's Symposium.

Therefore I've decided to mostly join Jeanne, and eat much less meat, so long as I don't have to go cold turkey.

Then the Lord said to Cain, "Where is Abel your brother?" He said, "I do not know; am I my brother's keeper?"

–Genesis 4: 9

JEANNE

DOCTOR

DECEMBER 12, 2013

ACA: Fix It

What are we waiting for, assembled in the public square?

The barbarians are to arrive today.

Why such inaction in the Senate?
Why do the Senators pass no laws?

A friend asked why I haven't written about the Obamacare fiasco. "You mean the Affordable Care Act?" I said.

"Whatever," he said, knowing he's won that battle already. The Republicans are good at nasty nomenclature, like "nattering nabobs of negativism." How about "neanderthal neocons of nitpicking"? (Fun, and we're only using the "n-words," which they're fond of.)

This is a fiasco half caused by technical incompetence and half by sabotage. In a split country, 50% of those who should be helping to implement it—governors, politicians, insurance execs—are trying to derail it. President Obama should have expected this, and appointed a lot better techies. Millions of people, including me, can hardly order a book on-line, not to mention a complicated insurance policy. In Republican-led states like Florida, applicants have to move around road blocks crouching in their way like defensive linebackers.

But here's the thing. In the long run, this fiasco doesn't matter: America *needs* universal health care. Period. We've been waiting, and we can wait some more while it gets fixed.

We're the wealthiest country in the world—we have over 13 million millionaires (389,000 in New York City alone!)—and more are sprouting like dandelions. At the same time, the number of poor people is growing faster, too. Who would have thought? Well . . .

Almost 49 million Americans live in poverty, with 47 million of them uninsured. Hunger's serious in this country—and in this county: 3890 homeless people live in Pinellas County. Large-hearted citizens in our own neighborhood are constantly collecting food for the hungry, but the single best thing we could do for these people is to get them insured under the Affordable Care Act.

To many Republicans, these people are lazy deadbeats living on our tax money (unlike subsidized millionaire farmers, and billionaires stacking their money overseas). Most of the poor are children or low-wage workers, and most of the others are sick; and thousands of the sick are veterans who got sick while fighting for their country.

One of the most memorable moments of my activities as St. Pete's Poet Laureate was when I led a poetry workshop for the homeless, in a windowless downtown room near St. Anthony's Hospital. All of their poems were sad, but one poem, written by a haggard rail-thin black veteran, broke my heart because it was so patriotic, a long list of what he had loved and lost, including his country. I thought, We've ruined this man, and abandoned him.

The GOP has been working fanatically to wreck and derail the Affordable Care Act, and along with that, eliminate programs like Food Stamps that really help real people. (Paul Krugman calls this "economic self-mutilation.") These people who are hurt are poor, uninsured and, if they had the energy to pull a lever, would probably vote Democratic, so it's a win/win for Governor Scott. But this is a technological glitch in a moral problem, and Obama needs to keep the techies focused until it works smoothly. It's already succeeding in states as different as California and Kentucky, so this can be done. Ignore the Tea Party's rantings, and keep those heads down.

The test is, does Uncle Sam still have a heart? Do we? Get out those stethoscopes. We've been waiting for decades.

> *Because the barbarians are to arrive today.*
> *What further laws can the Senators pass?*
> *When the barbarians come they will make the laws . . .*
> *Complete Poems of Cavafy,* Harcourt Brace & World, Inc.
>
> –both quotes from "Expecting the Barbarians" by Cavafy (1863-1933), from *The Complete Poems by Cavafy* (Harcourt, Brace and World, Inc.)

PINE CONE CHRISTMAS WREATH

DECEMBER 28, 2013

3 Christmas Limericks

1. *This problem is phrased hypothetically*
   and—as it rhymes—quite poetically
   "Stopping by Woods"
   might deliver the goods
   but just if you look alphabetically

We were surprised, but on the list of things our children remember from childhood, Christmas limericks are near the top. Our "kids," all in their 50's now, flew in from various far-flung exotic metropolises to spend Christmas in St. Petersburg, which is, after all, an "Arts Destination City"—though they think of it basically as a "Mom's Cooking Destination Kitchen." Of course, different versions of family stories arise, but they're pretty united about Christmas itself: they all remember the little folded limericks left in their stockings with hidden clues leading to a secret gift, usually a modest bill, though like Social Security it's gone up about 1½ % a year. Most of these poemlets are lost to time, or at least to attics, but a few recently surfaced, including the one above, which our son Pete once pulled out of his miniature stocking, strung with the others above our fireplace.

To solve this riddling limerick, Pete—a scientist—had to remember two things: One, that "Stopping by Woods on a Snowy Evening" is a poem by Robert Frost; and two, that unlike most of our bookshelves, the tall mahogany one in our living room is crammed with alphabetically ordered poetry books. He solved this one pretty quickly, finding a gift card on page 224 of *The Complete Poems of Robert Frost*, squeezed between Edward Field's *Counting Myself Lucky* and Roy Fuller's *Collected Poems*. (Fuller, not known much in America, was a slyly clear-eyed British poet, as in the opening of his "Follower's Song": *Oh to be simple and give the salute, / To be hopeful and happy, / For life to be sucked through the root / And the branches sappy . . .*)

When our children grew up and got married, their wives and husbands got pressed into this ritual, usually harried into confusion by contradictory hints from their extended family. Tim's wife, Aya (born in Tokyo), was studying French when she got this murky one:

> 2. *This present is hidden* en haut
>   *where your* beau-père *might scribble his* mots
>   *There's no one to blame*
>   *but still it's been framed*
>   *near the Seine or behind or below*

Aya had to know the French—*en haut* = upstairs, *beau-père* = father-in-law, and *mots* = words—in order to go up to the room where I write. There she found on the walls a lot of framed art works, one of which is an etching of a Parisian book stall, with Notre Dame in the background and a glimpse of a river between them. Aya, having been to Paris—probably walking by that exact stall—knew the river was the Seine, and found her present behind the etching. *Des bravos!*

These games are less embarrassing than they could be, because they're always accompanied by traditional cups of eggnog (*de rigueur*, Aya would say), lined up on our low cocktail table—bought in 1966 for $2 from Good Will, and later tiled by Jeanne—under our also traditional decorated tiny live tree, which we'd plant in the yard after the holidays. Now this *was* embarrassing while the children were students at Lakewood High School. They referred to it as our "annual Christmas bush," because (they claimed) their friends always asked, sarcastically, "Well, what kind of bush are you getting for a Christmas tree this year?" Fortunately, our charming handmade pine-cone Christmas wreath—made by Betty, my dad's third wife—generally went unnoticed as its colors blended into our brown front door.

But these little ditties were popular enough that they began to appear at other celebratory events, such as this one for our daughter Gretchen's high school graduation, when she found an envelope on her bed.

3. Today other girls get a Porsch
 a stereo a pearl or a horcsh;
  It's really embarrassing—
  We can hardly give anything
 (except for some casch but of corsch)

Happy Holidays to everyone! Eggnogsch all around!

2014

READING

JANUARY 9, 2014

Early Words

There is no Frigate like a Book
To take us Lands away
Nor any Courser like a Page
Of prancing Poetry —

When I was very young, I ran away from home, taking the BMT from Flatbush to Manhattan, where a kind policeman picked me up, wandering around the station at Eighth Avenue. I had no identification and about a dollar in change, but in those days every kid in Brooklyn knew his or her address and telephone number, singing a catchy jingle each morning that began *"Remember your name and address / and telephone number, too."* So before long, my distressed parents arrived to take me home, snatching out of my hands a paperback with a lurid cover that some policeman in the Station House had loaned me while I waited. He didn't think I knew how to read.

My reason for running away was both clear and murky—which I later discovered was also true of most adult crises. I had brown hair, my younger sister Pat was blonde, and a third brother or sister was on the way. Out of the blue (to stay in the spectrum) I announced at dinner one evening that if this new arrival had red hair, I was going to run away. My unbelieving father applauded. A few days later, on being told that our family now had a baby girl named Carol with a nice crop of red hair, I pulled on my jacket and headed off.

Later, we often wondered where I got that bizarre idea, and decided it must have been my love of the Brother Grimm's Fairy Tales, which, in our illustrated copy at least, seemed to associate red with danger—even Snow White had "lips as red as blood." Speaking generally, of course, that adventure and all others that followed came because of my reading.

I know my mother read to my sisters and me when we were growing up in Brooklyn in the 1930's. Although she didn't go to college, except for a few summers at Cornell, she became a certified school teacher and had a lovely, soothing voice (passed on to our redheaded younger sister Carol). I don't remember Mom (or Dad) teaching me specifically, but by the time I got to kindergarten I knew how to read.

I'm convinced that early reading would solve a lot of society's problems today, particularly the gaping split between the Haves and Have-nots. Early reading launches us into the world of imagination, taking us to Oz and Wonderland and England and Germany and China. We have a divided society, and that division is set early on. Poverty divides us, but multiple-pronged reading programs could help make us a mobile society again. Free children's books! How many free books would canceling an unwanted, unused, and unnecessary bomber purchase? Looking to create more jobs? How about Readers for Needy Children?

With good books in their formative years, most children can move past the stupid movies and tv that make us stupider, and into the arts, or at least better TV and movies! I'm not talking highfalutin here—but look around any museum, any theater, any art gallery, any symphony, any bookstore: you'll see a crowd of early readers, who developed their tastes starting with Mother Goose and Fairy Tales and moving through A. A. Milne's "Now We Are Six, " Robert Louis Stevenson's "A Child's Garden of Verses," Lewis Carroll's "Alice in Wonderland," Maurice Sendak's "Where the Wild Things Are," and the rest of the pantheon. Unlike gin (usually), reading is a productive addiction.

Education's the entrance, early reading's the key, and art is the house with many rooms that we all need to enter to live a decent life.

Even if you run away once in a while, just remember your name and address: you *can* go home again.

> *This Traverse may the poorest take*
> *Without oppress of Toll —*
> *How frugal is the Chariot*
> *That bears the Human soul.*

> –both quotes from #1263 by Emily Dickinson *(The Complete Poems of Emily Dickinson*, Little, Brown & Co., 1955)

JANET YELLEN

JANUARY 23, 2914

Year of the Woman

*Money, the long green,
cash, stash, rhino, jack
or just plain dough.*

*Chock it up, fork it over,
shell it out. Watch it
burn holes through pockets.*

Unlike a good man, a good woman isn't hard to find, but in today's odorous political stew, it's hard to get one appointed. By "good" I mean smart, strong, and imaginative enough to consider who gets harmed as well as who benefits from any decision. This may leave out Sarah Palin and Michele Bachmann, but in general women seem able to navigate these stormy waters better than men.

The new stream-lined filibuster rules will help get more qualified women through the Republican block in the Senate. It's a bit risky to restrict the filibuster, but since it's been gamed into an almost daily ploy, it was time for a change. This was the only way, for example, to get gifted women like Patricia Millett appointed to the federal appeals court for the District of Columbia.

They're all important, but these were just the background for the decision to replace Ben Bernanke with Janet Yellen as head of the Federal Reserve, America's central banking system—the first woman to crash through the glass ceiling of national high finance. Although, on paper, she's by far the most qualified person ever nominated for this position, the Heritage Foundation pressured Republicans to unite against her, calling all who might support her nomination "enemies" and "traitors." In the end, because of the change in rules, only 26 Senators (all Republicans) voted against her.

Although writing these columns has of course made me rich, I still feel more comfortable writing about poetry than money. But one thing I've noticed is that the influx of large numbers of women into poetry writing (they've always been the majority of poetry *readers*) has raised the level of "fellowship"—interesting word in this context—among poets. Women in all fields seem more skilled at cooperation than their male counterparts, who are still playing King of the Hill. Governor Christie, anyone?

President Obama tends to appoint moderates, but even so, Senator Mitch "100% Anti-Obama" McConnell fights every nomination. (In Yellen's case, McConnell wimpishly didn't vote, seeing they couldn't win with the new rules.) As a bonus to her own qualifications, Yellen offers a rare two-for-one opportunity: her husband is the Nobel prize-winning economist George Akerlof. I'd love to hear their dinner conversations (*Maybe cut back on the salt, dear, and tweak the butter*).

Yellen has stated that lowering unemployment is her major goal, backing the Fed's stimulus campaign and supporting regulation of business. The fact that, like me, she was born in Brooklyn probably means nothing ...

Suddenly, America's getting a long-delayed boost by turning to the capable women knocking on our various doors: the talented Natasha Trethewey is our current Poet Laureate; brilliant Mary Barra has just been made GM's first female CEO; closer to home, Florida A&M University recently appointed Elmira Mangum, formerly Vice President of Budget at Cornell University, to be its first female president.

Money's a hard subject (poetry's not for sissies, either) and we need toughness here, but there's no reason that a hard head can't work with a warm heart. Janet Yellen has already proved she's tougher than Ben Bernanke, standing up to Alan Greenspan when she was the vice chairwoman of the Fed, and predicting correctly that his laissez-faire policies would lead to the bursting real estate bubble and our long-lasting depression.

The "Head of the Fed" is a big position. An Asian friend has told us that in China this is the Year of the Horse ("those born in Horse Years are skilful with money"), but I'm thinking that in America 2014 will be the Year of the Woman.

> *It greases the palm, feathers the nest,*
> *holds heads above water,*
> *makes both ends meet . . .*
>
> *Money. You don't know where it's been,*
> *but you put it where your mouth is.*
> *And it talks.*
>
> –both quotes from "Money," by Dana Gioia, in *The Gods of Winter* (Graywolf Press 1991)

CAMPUS CHAPEL

FEBRUARY 6, 2014

Unhealthy Activities

Yes, the mouse you found
is broken snapped out of breath
by the copper rib and yes
we all break later or
sooner in the trap of death . . .

When I was in college, our fraternity (a compatible group of lively sinners) lived in a comfortable pub, known as the Deke house, not far below the College's famous three-storied chapel, with a three-faced clock keeping its twitching eye on us. We were told it was the only three-storied chapel in America, but none of us ever checked this out, being more interested in avoiding chapel than in researching historic architecture. Once—shortly before our time—the clock began ringing 13 times at noon, and students could get away with skipping required chapel because it was haunted. But after a while the puzzled building inspectors noticed some bright marks on the old bell: some sharp-shooting student was firing a .22 rifle from Middle Dorm, with perfect timing, through the small opening in the bell tower. The shooter—never identified—only fired at noon because, the story goes, he wasn't sober enough at midnight.

In the 1940s and 50s fraternities were built into college life, and the question wasn't "Would we join?" but "Which one?" Many of us, myself included, were used to this, having belonged to fraternities in high school. My high school fraternity seemed mostly like an Athletic Club, but my single specific memory of it involves a very bad evening.

Five of us were in a Jeep driven by a sixteen-year-old with no driver's license; in the other front seat his brother was warning him about the gravelly curve in front of our little town's railroad station. In the back seat, a blindfolded boy sat between me and another fraternity member. It was Initiation Night.

The car started to tip over in what seemed like slow motion. I had time to take off my glasses and slip them inside my shirt. The Jeep had a cloth top, and I could see the curb coming up toward my head, and right after that I blacked out. Apparently the car skidded on its side for thirty feet before hitting a lamppost and turning upside down.

Fate is fickle, punishing some and letting others off the hook completely. Among the five of us, not counting some spectacular bruises, there were only two broken bones (one arm, one leg), and one concussion (mine). The two youngest—the driver and the blindfolded initiate—had no serious injuries.

This memory floated up because, looking at the Chapel on my college calendar, I thought of The Three Things I Did When I was Young that I Didn't Want Our Sons to Do. I feel guilty, because I enjoyed all three: football, smoking, and fraternities.

I still have close friends from my fraternities, and always look forward to seeing them and laughing about the wild old days; and I remember how smoking got me through some tough and important times, including my Ph.D. oral exam at the University of Minnesota where my inquisitors also smoked, so at the end of my trial the room had the visibility of downtown Beijing at rush hour. And I still like to watch football, remembering our hopeless high school team, and the excitement of Saturday afternoons, charging madly downfield to almost certain defeat that seemed somehow totally worthwhile.

Our boys never joined a fraternity or smoked or played football, though they managed to break a few bones anyway; but I feel in general they're much healthier (not to mention bigger and stronger) than I've ever been. We wish them, and our daughters, long, healthy and happy lives. Jeanne and I gave up smoking around 1980, and have already lived longer than we thought we would (and longer than I deserve). I sometimes feel that the Chapel's twitching eye may still be on me, so I better watch my step. Or maybe it's that sharpshooter. He's out there somewhere.

> *On the other hand*
> *we do after all live forever*
> *till we die*
> *and after that*
> *who wants to live forever?...*

–both quotes from 'The Mouse You Found' by Peter Meinke, from *Trying to Surprise God*, U. of Pittsburgh Press 1981.

PANTS DOWN

FEBRUARY 20, 2014

Saving a Generation

Consider me
As one who loved poetry
And persimmons

—Masaoki Shiki (1867-1902)

In 1972, when the public schools of Neuchâtel, Switzerland, closed for summer vacation, the students marched through the streets with their teachers; and the whole town, including us, applauded and threw confetti as each class paraded by, students waving at their parents and friends.

In 1985, our son Tim went to Takamatsu, our "sister city" in Japan, to teach English in its high school for a year. Tim, a graduate of Lakewood High School, recalls one of his first surprises: When he entered the classroom, the students stood up and bowed.

Our other son, Pete, married a young doctor, Wei Chu, who had moved to New York from Taiwan when she was a teen-ager, and somehow managed to learn English, graduate from high school on time, and go straight through for her medical degree at Johns Hopkins University. "How did you do that?" we asked. "We were taught," she said, "the main thing in life was to get a good education—that's what we heard, so that's what we did."

St. Petersburg, one of America's "arts destination" cities, has been getting unwanted national attention because of the fight between two girls that broke out recently in Gibbs High School. This isn't typical behavior at Gibbs, which is one of Pinellas county's magnet schools for the Arts. Still, Gibbs had 76 student suspensions for fighting last year—that's more than one skirmish a week (just imagine how many fights were uncaught or unpunished).

But it's not the fight itself that's the most disturbing element: it's the children standing around watching it unfold, laughing, egging the battle on, taking photos, shouting obscenities, and ignoring the struggling teacher. This indicates a pattern so deep one's heart sinks in contemplating it, because it's not a classroom problem, it's a societal problem.

We don't have to romanticize nations—all are capable of evil behavior. In our own lifetimes we've had the German holocaust, the Japanese rape of Nanking, Cambodia's Khmer Rouge, China's bloody "Cultural Revolution," mass killings in communist Russia, French torture in Algiers, slaughters all over Africa, our own behavior at My Lai and Abu Ghraib. In stressful times, we're pushed to define the "others" as less than human. We have to recognize when this tendency tries to get a foothold; and right now our democracy needs to be very alert

A week after the incident at Gibbs, 200 teens "rampaged" through the Florida State Fair in Tampa. Both incidents are connected by attitude: these young people not only don't respect their teachers, they don't respect the police. They disobey their parents, and trash their neighborhoods and schools. Psychologists tell us that we're "set" at very early ages, so it's possible that this whole generation is lost (in groups; some strong individuals always break away). In this melting pot of a world, other countries are working hard to build national feelings of respect for others, and are investing huge resources in their schools. Our local situation's made extra complicated because most, though not all, of these young misbehavers are black, so our mayors, principals, and superintendents need to get black leaders involved. (I think even the well behaved young men in our neighborhood are in trouble, walking around with their underwear prominently displayed. I'm not sure what wearing your pants below your heinie declares, but it doesn't say Education First!)

To get hold of this problem, along with these pants, we have to start early and start small. Government programs to help young parents, especially single mothers. Higher pay and better training for teachers. Black and white leaders working together.

And maybe sometimes in the classroom, try a little poetry. Begin with reading and writing a simple haiku. It might help them to calm down, to look around at the seasons, the skies, the flowers. All you need to start is to be able to count to seventeen: 5+7+5 syllables. You don't have to write about persimmons (that's just a favorite of mine), and anybody can write one:

> *Gibbs High School students*
> *bloom like orchids in a storm*
> *bruised and beautiful*
>
> –haiku by Peter Meinke

YAMAZAKI

MARCH 3, 2014

Japanese Bourbon

Something there is that doesn't love a wall . . .

Our parents (fathers particularly) were disappointed when we traded in our all-American Dodge Coronet for a VW van. We were freezing in Minnesota, and the Dodge's power windows had stuck in the open position, its rusting tailpipe coughing like an old hot rod. When a friend bought a new Dodge Dart, I told him we had a Dodge, too, but it wasn't exactly a Dart.

By the time we'd worked our way through a few Toyotas to our current Honda, our dads had given up: it was too hard to tell what country owned what car, and even what parts of the car were made where. "At least we still have Jim Beam," a friend said one night, pouring another one.

Well, so much for that. Last month Japan's Suntory Company bought Beam, Inc., maker of Jim Beam and Maker's Mark bourbon, for sixteen billion dollars.

Americans know about Suntory from the 2003 movie, "Lost in Translation," where a fading actor (Bill Murray) goes to Tokyo because he's been offered two million dollars to make an ad for Suntory whiskey. The movie's a sad love story (involving Scarlet Johansson, the bone-melting voice in "Her"), but Murray's reluctant ad-making is hilarious.

We have a cheerier connection with Suntory, from the same year as the movie. On a glorious September morning in rural Virginia, I had a few celebratory drinks with a dignified gentleman named Teiichi Aoki, the uncle of our son's charming bride, Aya Aoki. Aya's relatives had flown in from Tokyo for the wedding, performed under a huge oak tree, surrounded by the Shenandoah mountains and guests from all over the world. Teiichi and I had spoken to the group, and though our verbal communication was limited, we agreed it was good to sit and quietly admire the handsome couple, toasting their future health and happiness. We clinked our glasses enough times to ensure their success.

That Christmas we received a package from Japan: a short warm note and a bottle of Suntory's gold-medal Yamazaki whiskey, which we received regularly for years, until Teiichi passed away in 2012. It's a fine whiskey, and I wish I could still sit with him, talking about the kids, and debating which is better, Yamazaki or Maker's Mark. It would be a long conversation.

Although rooted in the Kentucky hills, Maker's Mark, with its distinctively shaped bottle dipped in red wax, was introduced to me by a humorist from New York. I once was commissioned to interview Jean Shepherd, then living on Sanibel Island (where he died, in 1999). Years earlier, I'd been a fan of his long-running late night radio show on WOR, with its subversive wit—a precursor of both Jerry Seinfeld and John Stewart.

Anyway, the first words he said to me, rather abruptly, were, "Have you ever had Maker's Mark?" I recognized the name from ads—"The Ambassador of Bourbon"— but our budget hadn't allowed us to go above Jim Beam in price. I don't think the magazine ever published the interview, maybe because after an afternoon of listening and laughing (and sipping) my notes made little sense. I wrote to Shepherd not long afterward saying that I'd impulsively bought my first bottle of Makers Mark, after getting paid $50 in cash for a reading.

We really are citizens of the world, or should be. Jeanne and I don't drink Coca-cola—bad for our teeth—but its Super Bowl ad, sung in seven languages, was right on target. It's complicated, of course: boundaries make us feel safer; but in the long run, they don't work, as Robert Frost implies in his poem. Look around. Boundaries in all areas are falling: Down with walls! Good bourbon has brought much conviviality into this world; and will continue to do so, no matter who owns it.

I'll drink to that—maybe on St. Patty's Day. *Sláinte*, Jean! *Kampai*, Uncle Teiichi!

> *He moves in darkness, as it seems to me,*
> *Not of woods only and the shade of trees...*
> *He says again, "Good fences make good neighbors."*

–both quotes from "Mending Wall" by Robert Frost (1874-1963)

CHURCH OF SPILLED BLOOD

MARCH 20, 2014

Putin Rides the Wave

Ice is growing on the windowpanes.
The clock is repeating: "Don't be afraid!"
Hearing what is walking toward me,
I'd be afraid even if I were dead.

It was midnight in St. Petersburg, and I'd just read a poem on the radio. It was a call-in poetry program.

"It's midnight," I said in the silence that followed. "Who's listening to poetry at this hour, much less calling in?"

"Hey," my friend said. "Wait till you see. We're all crazy here."

The phones began to ring.

Ilia Foniakov smiled at me. This was St. Petersburg, Russia, and he was my translator.

Ilia died a few years ago, but I thought of his half-joking remark—*We're all crazy here*—as Putin raised the world's anxiety and sent his soldiers into Crimea. Does he want to start World War III? Are Russians really bonkers? Tennyson's famous poem about the charge of the Light Brigade during the Crimean War sprung to mind: *All in the valley of death . . .*

Earlier in the day, before the radio program, Jeanne and I had visited the novelist Dostoevsky's house, and then sat drinking coffee in the shadow of St. Petersburg's most exotic architectural glory, the Church of Spilled Blood, a huge intricate amalgam of colorful onion domes. Building it began in 1883, two years after Dostoevsky's death a short distance away (Czar Alexander II was assassinated on the site). A proper monument to the Russian spirit, the Church exudes an over-the-top passion that fuses religion with nationalistic fervor. I can easily imagine a Russian patriot, let's call him Rush Limbawksi, fulminating from its mosaic archways, urging its congregation to rise up against the infidels outside.

President Vladimir Putin, at 5'5" an inch shorter than Napoleon, exhibits some of the French emperor's aggressive traits, and may be willing to lead his country into similarly disastrous excursions. Putin's almost namesake, the mad mystic Rasputin, seemed temporarily untouchable, and Putin too seems impervious to threats. Like Napoleon, he's tactically shrewd and hard to beat, driven by his own self-regard, stung by supposed insults to himself from American and European leaders.

In his heart, he's riding the same wave as such disparate groups as the Islamists, al-Qaida and the Tea Party, a struggle of religious orthodoxy (in Putin's case, the Russian Orthodox Christian Church), against corrupt secular infidels—the less rational the belief, the more passionate the believers, which is their greatest advantage. Russia's fierce anti-gay vigilantes are known as "Putin's God Squad." (Back home last December, we received several Christmas cards that said "Season's Greetings," with notes from America's milder God Squad claiming that President Obama has forbidden us to say "Merry Christmas." Millions of Americans believe this stuff.)

I've always loved Dostoevsky's novels, which often do attack secular rationalism, sensing the shallowness and greed of modern commercial societies. But Putin has misread Dostoevsky the way Hitler misread Nietzsche, and the way the Tea Party misreads the Bible. They all pick and choose their favorite lines, out of context, and use them to attack others, ignoring the major message, which is "Look into yourselves and confess your own contradictions and imperfections." The answer, the wise ones seem to say, isn't to conquer infidels, but to talk to them and try to embrace them. Brothers and sisters alike, we're all shallow sinners. (Translated into practical terms: Squeeze Putin, without shootin'.) So far, Obama has the right idea.

To channel Dostoevsky's "underground man," I myself am embarrassed for wasting your valuable time with this essay. Let's put this foolishness aside and ponder our own lives in the shadow of the Church of Spilled Blood.

I beg the door as I would an idol:
"Don't let disaster in!"
Who is howling behind the wall, like an animal,
What is hiding itself in the garden?

–both quotes from 'Fragment,' by Anna Akhmatova (1889-1966), in *The Complete Poems of Anna Akhmatova*, translated by Judith Hemschemeyer, Zephyr Press, 1990.

JOHN DONNE

APRIL 3, 2014

Backward and Forward: John Donne

No man is an island, entire of itself; every man is a piece of the Continent, a part of the main . . .; any man's death diminishes me, because I am involved in Mankind; and therefore never send to know for whom the bell tolls; it tolls for thee."

Most American males reading the above probably think, "Wow, that Hemingway guy really could write!" But women are better read than men these days, so many of them (and some men) will remember it—*Meditation XVII*—was written by the English poet John Donne. His birthdate's disputed, but he died on March 31, 1631, which is one reason I'm thinking of him this week; though in truth, he's often on my mind in any case.

The sentence quoted above, with its quadruple repetition of "man," may irk a pure feminist, though Donne would be a tad less famous if he'd written, "No man or woman is an island, entire of himself or herself." But Donne was speaking the language of his day; and anyone who's read his poetry would understand that he loved women in general, and his wife Anne in passionate particular. A true and turbulent love story: Donne and Anne More married in 1601 against everyone's wishes. In those politically and religiously dangerous days, this cost him his court appointment, and he was thrown into Fleet Prison in London, writing in a letter to her, "John Donne; Anne

Donne; Un-done." Although his brilliant eloquence (and conversion from Catholic to Anglican) led him to be pardoned, and later made Dean of St. Paul's Cathedral, his poems remained unpublished until after his death.

None of this I knew when I was taking a class at Hamilton College from Professor Robert Rudd, aka fondly as Bobo. (All popular Hamilton profs had nicknames, *e.g.*, "Digger" Graves, "Swampy" Marsh, "Shifty" Gere *et al.*) Bobo, an elderly, distinguished scholar, had just recited from memory Shakespeare's Sonnet #73, *"That time of year thou mayst in me behold / When yellow leaves, or none, or few, do hang / Upon those boughs which shake against the cold, / Bare, ruin'd choirs, where late the sweet birds sang . . .,"* his scratchy voice shaking with emotion. On the spot, I—a closet poet—decided to enclose two poems with the essay written for Bobo's class. Though I loved poetry, my inexperienced teen-aged self had never heard it read like that before.

In our next class, Professor Rudd returned my poems with no comment, except to print out, GO BUY THE SELECTED POEMS OF JOHN DONNE. That afternoon I found it in the college book store, part of the diminutive Laurel Poetry Series with muscular portraits by Richard Powers on its covers. It was the first book of poetry I ever bought, costing 40 cents. Of course tuition was about $600 a semester, so money back then spoke a different language; and it wasn't long before I had the whole series. Poet Richard Wilbur, whom I'd meet much later, was the General Editor

They say we always remember our first love, and the same may be true in poetry—my previous affection for Poe turned out to be puppy love. I stayed up all night reading Donne's poems, not clear on much of their meaning, but understanding that this was the kind of poetry I'd want to write if I knew how: smart, passionate, sexy, and witty, compressed into complex shapes and rhyme schemes. The poems were challenging, and worth the work—something I can't say of some of the perplexing poems I try to read today.

No matter what we do or make or believe, all of us, famous or unknown, stand on the shoulders of those who went before us; life is, as a friend wrote recently, "a web of dependencies." We dangle in the middle, thankful for those who helped us, hoping to touch some of those who come after. People, like poems, look backward and forward at the same time.

Verse hath a middle nature: heaven keeps souls,
The grave keeps bodies, verse the fame enrolls.

–from "An Anatomy of the World" by John Donne

POPE FRANCIS

APRIL 17, 2014

A Kinder Pope

The perpendiculars of our world
Are at odds with one another:
Spruce-boles & boat-masts spar;
Also dock-pier pillars . . .

Like everyone else, we're happy to have a pacific face smiling from the Vatican. From the very beginning, when the Argentine bishop Jorge Mario Bergoglio became the first Pope Francis, his choice of the humble saint of Assisi for his name suggested a turn in direction from Pope Benedict XVI, whose résumé and name choice reaffirmed the pomp and circumstance of the Vatican hierarchy.

Pope Benedict, when he was Cardinal Joseph Ratzinger, had acquired the unfortunate nickname of "the Pope's Rottweiler," and it's difficult for even a Pope to shake off an alliterative and Dickensian nickname like Rottweiler Ratzinger. (In his pre-Popean days, he was known as a strict enforcer of orthodoxy, silencing many of the more liberal priests in the Church and—what became important later—obstructing inquiries about the Church's sex abuse scandal.)

Although Pope Benedict at 87 is a decade older than Pope Francis, it's not age that caused his resignation, which caught almost everyone by surprise. Instead, it was his inability to handle the hypocrisy within the Church, which had been long rumored, and brought to murky light by a report stamped "Pontifical Secret" and leaked to Italian journals. The culprit behind these "VatiLeaks" wasn't WikiLeaker Edward Snowden but—like a grade B crime novel—

the butler, Pablo Gabriele, the Pope's personal manservant. In a sensational trial, Gabriele was convicted of "aggravated theft," and soon pardoned by Benedict. The Pope wasn't implicated himself, but the scandal and turmoil escalated, involving accusations of money laundering, widespread corruption, and homosexuality, the daily reports and rumors reading like the script of America's hit political series, "House of Cards."

Into this Roman feeding frenzy stepped Pope Francis, with his soft voice and shy (but sly) smile. "Wretched are those who are vindictive and spiteful," he said. "If someone is gay who searches for the Lord and has goodwill, who am I to judge?" And more lightly, "I love tango, and I used to dance when I was young." How can you not like him?

Compared to previous Popes, Francis is letting in some sun—and sunlight might in time lead to action. In addition, he's touchingly warm to his conflicted predecessor, Benedict, living nearby. Francis, like his namesake, the patron saint of animals, seems to even love rottweilers.

The shadow—-where there's sunlight there's always a shadow—is that not only do the poor and liberals love Pope Francis, but the rich and conservatives love him too. Rick Santorum—who has compared homosexuality to man-on-dog sex—loves him. This should make us nervous. "What he's doing is the right thing," Santorum says. John Boehner has invited Francis to speak to Congress.

So far, at least, Pope Francis *has* said the right things, but as yet hasn't changed any of the Church's actual practices. Until he, or it, does, women will remain second-class citizens with its patriarchal stand against birth control; and poor families will remain poor, with its stand on abortion; and the rich (Hobby Lobby comes to mind) will continue to donate huge amounts of their tax-supported money to the forces that keep it that way.

Nevertheless, the Pope's gentle and forgiving voice is a gift of grace in a harsh world. Some have complained he has yet to give orders to his troops, but the Pope isn't a general: he's a leader by example. Like Gandhi, he sends out signals with his public behavior. Who can tell what will come of this? Perhaps, at this Easter-time anyway, this is all that can be done.

So, good health and long life to Pope Francis; and Happy Easter, everyone!

What wright is capable of right-wising
Things tilting, collapsing, & capsizing,
Except encompassing compassion?

–both quotes from "Ecstatic Task of the Eschaton" by Tony Stoneburner (in "Gatherings," published by Limekiln Press, Granville, Ohio, 1997)

RUSSELL CROWE AS NOAH

MAY 1, 2014

Wipeout

And the Lord was sorry that he had made man on the earth, and it grieved him to his heart. So the Lord said, "I will blot out man whom I have created from the face of the ground, man and beast and creeping things and birds of the air, for I am sorry that I made them." But Noah found favor in the eyes of the Lord.

–from Genesis 6:6-8

When I was a boy—a faithful attendee of Sunday School in our neighborhood Lutheran Church—I loved the Bible stories, which we read, and were read to us, in variant renditions of our Brooklyn accents: "And rain fell upon da oith fawty days and fawty nights . . ." (Almost every day our teachers in grade school—P.S. 222 on Quentin Road—made us recite a poem, designed to cure our accents, that began "There once was a *turtle* / Whose *first* name was *Myrtle* . . ." But . . . *fuhgeddaboudit!*)

My interest in these stories intensified when I discovered on my parents' bookshelf a heavy bible illustrated by Gustav Doré, which featured, in Noah's story, a drowning family clinging to a sharp rock. A muscular naked man held his voluptuous naked wife above the water, while their naked children shared the small space on the rock with a huge tiger holding her cub in its mouth. I learned early on that most artists were fascinated by nudity. So was I. Oddly enough, the scene resembled the stony volcanic landscape of the recent movie, "Noah," filmed in Iceland instead of the Mideast.

Like any good story, the Biblical one is very specific in places: *In the six hundredth year of Noah's life, in the second month, on the seventeenth day of the month, on that day all the fountains of the great deep burst forth, and the windows of the heavens were opened.* In the movie, Director Darren Aronofsky follows some of the crazy specifics, like the size and shape of the ark; and where the Bible is vague, he puts in his own crazy specifics, like huge creatures called the Watchers, apparently made out of rocks and appointed by God to protect the ark from invaders. When the polluters of the earth, namely all mankind, try to attack Noah and get on his ark, these creatures rise out of the stony landscape and smite the sinners by the thousands, reminiscent of some of Arnold Schwarzenegger's Terminator sci-fi fantasies.

We can see what attracted Aronofsky. The last movie we saw of his was "Black Swan," in which Natalie Portman plays a ballet dancer whose intensity morphs into madness and her body bleeds as she turns into the black swan, wings breaking out of her back. It's a mix of fairy tale and horror movie, and "Noah" shows the same combination, but in a larger Biblical, or epic, proportion.

The "problem" with Noah's story, of course (at least if taken literally) is the idea of God wiping out the whole world, but the movie takes this head-on. In "Noah," the world's been polluted by man (there's a background shot suggesting smokestacks and today's looming environmental disasters), but still, drowning everyone but Noah's family and a few animals seems a bit much.

Not only that, Noah, played by a slightly puffy Russell Crowe, takes God's orders to the extreme, deciding his job isn't to save sin-cursed man, but just the "clean" animals; and is prepared to do away with his whole family in a very dramatic ending. (The movie catches some of the Bible's drama but not much of its poetry.)

I've always felt distressed about our atomic bombing of Hiroshima and Nagasaki—all those women and children!—and the same questions arise here. Even Methuselah, Noah's grandpa (wittily played in "Noah" by Anthony Hopkins), didn't have answers, apparently dying in the nick of time, just before the Flood.

But Noah had a long time to think about them:

After the flood Noah lived three hundred and fifty years. All the days of Noah were nine hundred and fifty years; and he died.

–from Genesis 9:28

WALTER CRONKITE

MAY 29, 2014

Mayday

Turning and turning in the widening gyre
The falcon cannot hear the falconer;
Things fall apart; the centre cannot hold;
Mere anarchy is loosed upon the world...

Recently I opened up the Tampa Bay Times to the editorial pages and saw three headlines: DEMOCRACY PUT UP FOR SALE (the editorial), GAP IN WEALTH IS EVEN WIDER THAN WE THOUGHT (Jordan Weissman), and LEGISLATORS ROLL OVER, FETCH FOR BIG UTILITIES (Daniel Ruth).

My first thought was, "Well, duh, everybody's heard this." My second was "Mayday!"—because everyone *hasn't* heard it; or if they have, they don't believe it. (For those not familiar with distress calls, "Mayday"—from the last two syllables of the French phrase *Venez m'aider*: Help me!—is the international signal, usually repeated three times, for life-threatening emergencies.)

The above articles were detailed and well written. They told us to pay attention to the assaults being made on our democracy by legislators, business leaders, and Supreme Court justices.

But headlines like these are shouting into a void. Newspapers, fading away as the makers of public opinion, have fired a fifth of their reporters, and television reporting has splintered like a kaleidoscope. The result is that these excellent articles aren't read by enough people, blotted out by contrary voices and false advertisements on the other media outlets. In this environment obvious truths—like climate change, widespread voter restrictions, and the chasm between America's rich and poor—become not only less obvious, but subject to endless debate. No consensus means no action, to the detriment of America's democracy, health, and once enviable future.

This change took less than 40 years to happen.

In 1981 Walter Cronkite, commonly called "the most trusted man in America," retired, lining up neatly with the election of Ronald Reagan, once the star of "Bedtime for Bonzo," and a supporter of Barry Goldwater. In the decades before Reagan's rule, the U.S. had become the beacon of the world with its courage, generosity, and prosperity. Our public education was matchless, workers were paid well, the GI bill built the middle class, unions flourished, Social Security solidified, and taxes were fair (the rich, as in most countries, paid a lot more—but still had a lot more than everyone else). The "Greatest Generation," basically World War II through the Civil Rights laws, powered America to the forefront of the world (my group, the "Silent Generation"—I apologize, softly—was the buffer zone between the Greatest and the Boomers).

These programs passed because, despite loud dissenters, the country as a whole could follow the debates, and make up its mind. Besides Cronkite on CBS Evening News (preceded by the tougher Edward R. Murrow on radio), there were Chet Huntley and David Brinkley on NBC, and Harry Reasoner on ABC, all sober and serious voices. This was far from perfect. Where were minorities? Where were women? (Barbara Walters joined Reasoner eventually). But these voices all fell within an agreed-upon range of normality, integrity and civility—and things got done.

I don't want to blame the affable Reagan for everything, but our invasion of Grenada in 1983 (Operation Agent Fury) was a sign of things to come. Hate groups, energized by President Obama's election, are rising sharply. Fury, instead of civility, marks our social and political discourse—*You lie!*—echoing 1939 Germany, an educated

Christian country which followed the loudest voice yelling the biggest lies.

America's proved it can be resourceful in times of crisis, so I'm not despairing. But with this wealth gap boosted by recent Supreme Court decisions; and climate change action already decades behind; and our racial problems rattled by recent voting rights and affirmative action setbacks, we should all be nervous.

But not silent: Mayday! Mayday! Mayday!

> *And what rough beast, its hour come round at last,*
> *Slouches towards Bethlehem to be born?*
>
> –both quotes from "The Second Coming," from *The Collected Works of W.B Yeats, Volume I,* Scribner 1997.

MARTINI WITH GREEN OLIVES

JUNE 12, 2014

Happy Fathers

My father's eyes rolled upward in Paul's Diner
not in fine frenzy but diabetic coma
and we thought when they refocused two weeks
later it was time to make amends . . .

Jeanne's and my fathers were old-style Republicans. High school graduates from blue-collar backgrounds, they worked hard, and eventually prospered as salesmen, Jeanne's dad (Roger) owning his own real estate business, and mine (Harry) becoming a manufacturer's rep for metal products in New Jersey.

Big loving good-natured guys who enjoyed a drink (and a few more), they were proud to send their children to college, which had some unpredictable results; the first being that Jeanne and I fell in love while she was at Syracuse and I was at nearby Hamilton. When I finished my Army service in 1957, we got married, and our fathers wanted us to work for them so we could prosper as they had.

Perversely, it seemed we both had a mutated gene, and quickly displayed an allergy to selling anything, sales ability bouncing off us whenever an opportunity approached. Neither Jeanne nor I could sell a mitten to an Eskimo.

Still, they hoped we'd learn, and were disappointed when we jumped ship for the academic life. We drove off to the University of Michigan with two toddlers and two thousand dollars, while they rolled their eyes and worried. But something even worse than poverty awaited us: We became Democrats.

On September 26, 1960, Jeanne and I sat in a fellow graduate student's apartment and watched the Nixon/Kennedy debate—we had no TV—and it changed our lives. Of course, that debate changed many other things in the world, but before long our politics, always a bit unfocused, took a sharp left turn.

Our practical fathers handled this by ignoring politics entirely and, whenever it flared up, treated it as a transient disease, like mumps. Our mothers kept silent, but we suspected these talented introspective women were secretly sympathetic to our cause.

A typical incident: In the 60's hair was a big issue, a dividing line. In 1969, on the way to teach a summer class in England, we flew out of the Newark NJ airport, and stopped by to see Roger and Ruth (Jeanne's mother). My hair was a little long and I was sporting a slipshod Trotskyesque goatee. That night, Roger looked hard at me and said, "Don't come back again until you get a proper haircut." We took off for England the next morning.

On the plane I said, "You realize, I can't cut my hair any more."

Jeanne didn't have to think about it. "I guess not."

Two months later, when we flew back to Newark, I was a lot shaggier than when we left. Hugs all around, celebrations, and reunion with the kids. Roger never mentioned my hair again—he seemed to have forgotten his remark—and pretty soon, back in Florida, I shaved and got a haircut, keeping the moustache.

That's what I meant by "old-style Republicans." They had the same basic opinions as the others, but over the years, as the Meinke/Clark family tree sprouted to include Jewish, Catholic, Muslim, Black, Chinese, Japanese and gay members along its branches, these old white guys stepped up to the plate and welcomed all of us home. Of course, along the line, when we told them we were going to Poland for a year, they brought out their Polish jokes. They were Republicans we could love; and we did.

As for my dad, after his doctor forbade him to drink, his wife

Betty allowed Harry one martini whenever Jeanne and I came to visit; so he said he was always happy to see us, even if we *were* Democrats. He let me make the martinis; he had taught me how. As the old saying goes, the olive doesn't fall far from the tree.

> *. . . and let me tell you old man I was proud*
> *at having the strongest father on the block*

> –both quotes from "Father," in *Liquid Paper: New & Selected Poems*, by Peter Meinke, U. of Pittsburgh Press (1991)

GRETA GARBO

JULY 3, 2014

Unsmiling

Greta Garbo Poem #25

When I'm with Greta Garbo
she gets very talkative
She likes me to put on my Russian accent
and she plays Ninotchka again
People think we're crazy
especially the waiters at Howard Johnson's
Do you want dessert? they ask
Oh no says Greta Garbo
Ve vant to be alone!
and she & I laugh and laugh and laugh

Actually, the movies' greatest film star later claimed she never said that (though I was there, as the waiters will attest). She said she meant to say "I want to be *let* alone," though in Greta Garbo's case, both seem to be applicable. She never married, but was loved by both men and women, and occasionally reciprocated to both, remaining, like Churchill's Russia, a "riddle wrapped in a mystery inside an enigma."

She was born in 1905, in Stockholm, so in 1969 she was 64 (it's very hard to think of Greta Garbo as an older woman). In that year, Jeanne and I were living in the village of Falmer, England, near the vacation town of Brighton, with its famous boardwalk and the exotic Royal Pavilion where King George IV partied with his friends and mistresses. We'd been traveling with sixteen Eckerd students, taking them on their continental education through Florence, Munich, Amsterdam, London, Lucerne, and Paris, before settling down at the University of Sussex for some serious teaching and study time (I was lecturing on Chaucer's *Canterbury Tales*, and a visit to Canterbury Cathedral was on our agenda). By sheer luck, we'd gone almost directly from seeing the Mona Lisa at the Louvre to a Greta Garbo movie festival at the University.

This was educational in many ways. As we sat through "Anna Christie," "Anna Karenina," "Camille," and "Ninotchka" on successive evenings, we decided Greta Garbo was the Mona Lisa of movie stars—or perhaps the Mona Lisa is the Greta Garbo of famous portraits: both of them mesmerizing, not quite smiling, and ineffably calm. In that sixteenth century masterpiece—we learned—Leonardo da Vinci invented the *sfumato* technique, a blending of light and shade that emphasized the eyes and mouth, which in Mona Lisa's portrait makes her both expressive and unknowable. And those are exactly the traits we remember when we think of Greta Garbo.

Americans have to smile so much! We're bombarded by ads for whitening toothpaste, electric toothbrushes and aggressive waterpicks that promise to make us look more desirable as we smile at the birdie. Our "pursuit of happiness" has morphed from a right to a responsibility, and we worry if we don't feel, and look, happy as a little doggie.

So, after seeing all those magical movies, with those serious eyes magnified on the screen in Sussex, Jeanne and I perceived that neither Greta nor Mona would ever smile at the birdie; and we resolved never again to smile unnecessarily. Whenever we entered a room where people waited for us, we vowed to remain dignified, unsmiling, and—yes!—mysterious. We could practice this with the English, whose dignity, though eroding along with the Royal Family, is still at a higher level than found in the average American living room, where grins pop like paparazzi flashbulbs. Alas, try as we might, as soon as we set foot in a room, or a camera pointed its lewd eye toward us, we felt the corners of our lips turning up against our will, distending into a desperate grimace. Charlie! Maggie! How're you doin'?

Greta! Mona! Help!

> *Are you warm, are you real, Mona Lisa*
> *Or just a cold and lonely, lovely work of art?*
>
> –from the song "Mona Lisa" by Ray Evans and Jay Livingston (1950)

"Greta Garbo Poem #25," by Peter Meinke, is from *The Contracted World: New & More Selected Poems*, U. of Pittsburgh Press (2006)

TRAFFIC JAM

JULY 10, 2014

Stuck with Traffic

Once my nose crawled like a snail on the glass;
my hand tingled
to burst the bubbles
drifting from the noses of the cowed, compliant fish . . .

We had a 4 pm meeting at the Tampa Museum of Art, and as we nosed into the traffic on the Howard Frankland Bridge, we joined the cars dragging themselves across the Bay, and I thought of the Loggerhead turtles who lurch up the beaches near Fort De Soto every summer. (A bale of turtles = a jam of cars.) Like them, we're awkward and out of our element, but at least they get to lay their eggs.

How can so many people go through this every day? From our side on the Howard Frankland, it appears that equal amounts of cars are driving from each direction. In this new economy of two full-time breadwinners per family, many couples have to work on different sides of the Bay. (Actually, we saw this phenomenon a long time ago, when we lived in St. Paul—but to get to Minneapolis you just had to cross Snelling Avenue, not a seven-mile bridge.)

Now, our car stuck like a bill in Congress, Jeanne and I discussed starting a marriage exchange (EcoHarmony?) where bi-county couples commuting in opposite directions could hook up with compatible partners who work on the same side of the Bay, retaining home visiting rights for the weekend when traffic is lighter. This could be economical (save time), ecological (save gas), and even a little surprising now and then.

It's either that, or handle it like Poles in the 1970's. The Communist economy was so bad, Polish couples were often forced to take jobs in distant cities, so as I traveled out from Warsaw giving readings in various universities (Gdańsk, Poznań, Łódź, Krakow, *et al.*) we'd occasionally meet the husband or wife of new friends who lived in Warsaw. The Poles were both resilient and witty; when we'd commiserate, one might give us a sly wink and say, "Hey, every weekend's a honeymoon, OK?" And travel back and forth—by train of course—was pleasant and cheap.

It's amazing what we'll put up with. Once, after someone had wondered why all the poor in third world countries don't revolt, a friend said, "Oh, they're used to living like that." We don't think that's true, but then we're astonished to read that so many people still plan on voting for Governor Scott after his rejection in 2011 of government funds for high speed rail in Florida, and his constant preference for building roads and bridges instead of any kind of rail—unless it benefits his cronies. (He now supports a private passenger rail project from Miami to Orlando called All Aboard Florida, overseen by a company that used to employ his chief of staff, according to a Tampa Bay Times/Miami Herald report last month.)

Scott, along with Senator Marco Rubio, doesn't believe in man-assisted climate change—or else he just won't do anything President Obama thinks is a good idea—so the money (two billion dollars!) was reallocated, making Florida's Tea Party happy, and commuters in California and the Northeast Corridor a lot more comfortable.

A vote for Scott is a vote for four more years of ignoring climate change, increasing pollution (which intensifies the violence of our storms) and ensuring that our painful traffic jams will grow like cancer cells, eating up our highways. Charlie Crist has changed his views as he retools himself into a Democrat, but there's no doubt about the difference here: Crist will at least try to protect Florida's once pristine environment. With Scott in the pockets of Big Oil, fracking will sprout around us, oil will seep into our treasured Everglades, and the Howard Frankland Bridge will tremble as cars sit panting in the heat like the great sea turtles before they went extinct.

Sometimes poets really are prophets: Robert Lowell published the lines beginning and ending this column in 1964.

> *The Aquarium is gone. Everywhere,*
> *giant finned cars nose forward like fish;*
> *a savage civility*
> *slides by on grease.*

> –both quotes from "For the Union Dead," by Robert Lowell, from *For the Union Dead,* from The Noonday Press, New York (1972)

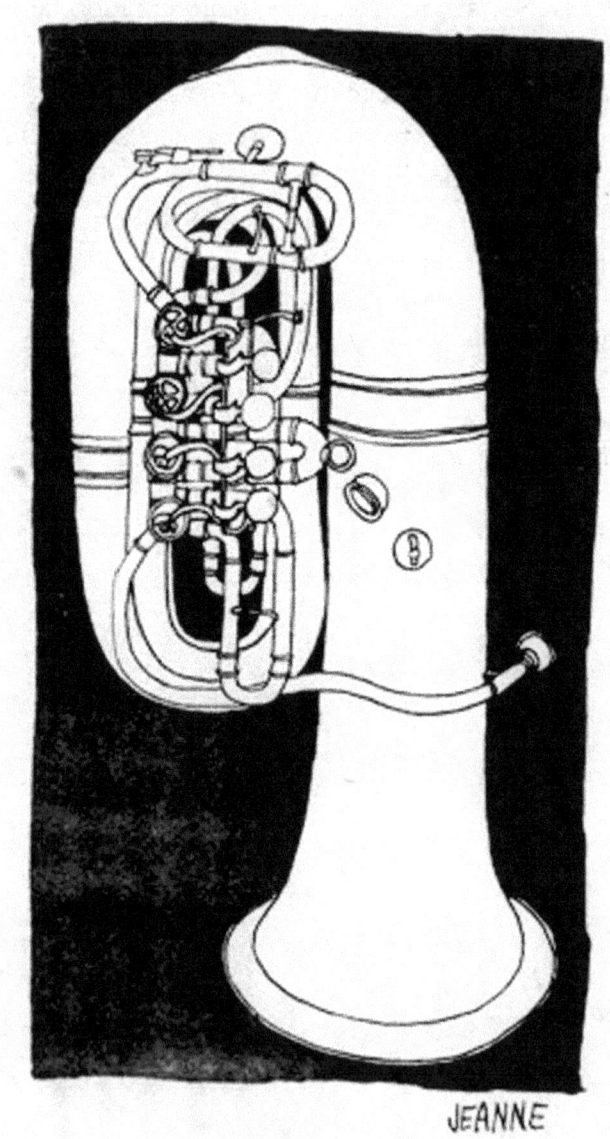

TUBA

JULY 24, 2014

Poetry & Music

"Sir, what is poetry?"
"Why Sir, it is much easier to say what it is not. We all know *what* light *is; but it is not easy to* tell *what it is."*

—Samuel Johnson, from Boswell's *Life of Samuel Johnson* (1791)

Although Dr. Johnson's right—poetry's slippery to define—we *can* say it's the form of writing closest to music: what's most important in poetry isn't plot, character, or setting, but sound and voice. As soon as that's said, you can think of poems that don't sound musical at all. (You can even think of some *music* that doesn't seem musical.) And in both cases, readers and listeners won't agree on their specific examples: John Cage; hiphop? *De gustibus non est disputandum*, the Latin to my ears more musical than "There is no disputing about taste."

All poets love music, lean on it and learn from it, whether it's Bach or the Beatles or Jacques Brel. I used to play the piano (not well, but often, at the cocktail hour), and recently submitted, successfully, to an operation on my right hand so I could play again (not well, and even worse). My fingers had curled up from an inherited condition called Dupuytren's Contracture. I like the name, pronounced "deP-WEEtrens conTRACture"—a double amphibrach. Every vocation has its own language, and in poetry an amphibrach is a three-syllable "foot," or metrical unit, with the middle syllable accented, as in limericks: "The LEGend ofLARry the LIZard / is CHAMpi on

SUper andWIZard" are the opening lines of one of Jeanne's and my charming unknown works, about a musical band of lizards, all much more talented than I am on the piano, told in a sequence of 40 limericks ("clean limericks": these days an oxymoron).

Some poets, perhaps to gather a little internal rhythmical capital, compose their poems while listening to music, though their choices are often surprising. Hart Crane liked writing to the thumping strains of Maurice Ravel's *Boléro*, pacing about his room as he did so. Today *Boléro* would just be distracting, familiar as the background music during Bo Derek and Dudley Moore's erotic love scenes in the smash movie, "10" (the ensuing sales of "Boléro" making the composer's descendents very rich, too late for Ravel himself; it has always been thus.)

Poetry began in song, and abandons it at its own peril. For centuries, poets have been fond of St. Cecilia, the patron saint of music. In 1687 John Dryden, Poet Laureate of England, wrote his famous "Song for St. Cecilia's Day," written to be accompanied by music, and beginning "From harmony, from heavenly harmony / This universal frame began." In a magical partnership, the music for it was written by England's greatest composer at the time, Henry Purcell. (A bit later, Paul Simon's "Cecelia" was a big hit in the 1970's.) Music and words together can slide through our hearts like a penknife through a peach; it's a common experience, after a poetry reading, to feel you've been deeply stirred (not shaken), but can't quite remember why.

Music isn't everything in a poem, of course. A good poem requires sense as well as sound. W. H. Auden said that Alfred Lord Tennyson "had the finest ear of any English poet, but was also the stupidest," perhaps channeling George Bernard Shaw who claimed that Tennyson "had the brains of a third-rate policeman." It can be nasty up there, where the air is thin.

Still, it's endearing to imagine the young Hart Crane, escaping to New York from priggish Ohio and, bursting with inspiration and Cutty Sark, leaping up from his table as the tuba solo from *Boléro* kicks in, leaning over to write the beginning of his great saga about the Brooklyn Bridge looming just outside his window, and farther down in New York Harbor the magnificent Statue of Liberty, arm upraised, welcoming this small-town boy to a strange new world where anything could happen.

> *How many dawns, chill from his rippling rest*
> *The seagull's wings shall dip and pivot him,*
> *Shedding white rings of tumult, building high*
> *Over the chained bay water Liberty —*
>
> –from "The Complete Poems of Hart Crane," Doubleday Anchor Books (NY 1958)

GINGERBREAD CASTLE

AUGUST 7, 2014

Accidental Lives

... because his father asked
which way was west because his father found
the sea a way of life because his father met
in hannover a buxom peasant girl ...

For over four decades Jeanne's been making gingerbread constructions, admired by the neighborhood. By now it's a family tradition—but it all started by accident.

One of Robert Frost's useful ideas is that one key to writing poetry is the ability to take advantage of happy accidents—those words and images that pop up from "the path less traveled by." The importance of chance is underestimated in our society, especially by the well off who believe those c-notes in their piggy banks are predestined because of their hard work and unflagging patriotism. But in discussions with friends, it's clear that many of our major decisions—where we live, whom we marry, number of children, "chosen" profession—wouldn't have happened if not for some unplanned event: A flat tire caused a chance meeting that led to a happy marriage, a rainstorm made someone duck into a store that changed her life, a book found on a park bench led to another book that would never have been read—and a new world opened up. In 1968 Jeanne discovered Driftwood only because she noticed a car-pooling acquaintance's car wouldn't start, and offered to take her child home from pre-school. Later, Jeanne said, "I've just seen a magical neighborhood."

Two years later, I was busy teaching at Florida Presbyterian College, a husband and father of four lively children, in no way thinking of leaving our newly found cottage in Driftwood. For one thing, we couldn't afford to visit our relatives in New Jersey, much less fly to Europe to see Big Ben or the Eiffel Tower. Besides, we had comfortable routines; and one of mine was 10 a.m. coffee with German Professor Ken Keeton, after our 9 o'clock classes.

One morning I was in his office, waiting for Ken to get off the phone, and casually picked up a stapled booklet from his desk: the AMFC Newsletter (AMFC, I saw, stood for Association of Mid-Florida Colleges). Flipping pages, thinking of nothing but coffee, I spotted a small announcement because it was outlined in black: *Wanted: Someone fluent in French to supervise 18 French majors at the University of Neuchâtel.* Apparently, no French professor in the entire state had volunteered.

I stared at the notice, reading again the phrase "someone fluent in French," and found myself murmuring (untruthfully, based on a few French courses in high school and college), "*C'est moi!*" I wrote down the address of the committee at Stetson College in Deland.

I won't repeat the story of the ups and downs of how this came to pass, but because of an off-hand glance in Ken's office—because a student had phoned just as I walked in—the six Meinkes eventually found ourselves on the train from Geneva, staring wide-eyed at the slanted rooftops and elfin turrets along Lake Neuchâtel.

It was also accidental that about two miles away from our Swiss home was a small stone castle, with twin turrets. Jeanne's Frostian inspiration was to look at those turrets and see them as made of chocolate—and remembering she had a funnel in her kitchen drawer exactly that shape. How did she get that idea? Maybe it was our new address—*Quai Suchard 12*—or maybe the wind was right, blowing through our neighborhood from the Suchard chocolate factory above Neuchâtel, and suddenly the gingerbread castle above appeared to her as if already done; and all the others were to follow . . .

Maybe everything *is* by accident, but not all taste so good.

... down
     we   *..*
       whirl
the docketing hill all slanted on
 our narrow sloping trace
chains of lowercase letters gone
before we reach what seems like space

when poles from frozen hands are flung
pens for stories in a broken tongue ...

 –both quotes from 'The Skiers" by Peter Meinke, in
 The Contracted World: New & More Selected Poems,
 U. of Pittsburgh Press 2006

BIER STEIN

AUGUST 21, 2014

On Foreign Shores

Deutschland, Deutschland, über alles,
Über alles in der Welt ...
(Germany, Germany, over all,
Above all in the world ...)

> –from *Das Deutschlandlied*, German national anthem, music by Franz Joseph Haydn, lyrics by August Heinrich Hoffman von Fallersleben (1841). These opening lines were first banned by the Allies in 1945, and then forbidden by the German government in 1952.

When I heard this stirring music, written by the great composer Haydn, played over and over as the German team marched through the World Cup, two thoughts repeated in my mind. One, the American team did pretty well, losing to the Germans by the same score as Argentina in the championship match (1-0).

The second was a memory from 1956, when I was a soldier stationed in Germany. One afternoon after we got off duty, two friends and I drove over the old bridge crossing the Main River up to a 13th century castle, Fortress Marienberg, just outside Würzburg. We'd done this before, sitting at a table by the ancient walls, drinking beer, watching the sun set over the town's lovely old turrets, domes and spires. But this time—we got off a little late, and didn't have time to change—we were still wearing our uniforms. Below us a barge floated by, carrying a huge red sign: *Trink Coca-Cola*.

We were feeling good: young, healthy, enjoying an adventure in a foreign country. Out of sheer exuberance, showing off our little German and clinking our large beers, we stupidly began singing *Deutschland, Deutschland, über alles*... Before we got to the third line, we heard chairs scraping on the cobblestones. Across the courtyard, not far behind us, a group of husky drinkers—possibly the Würzburg soccer team—had stood up and were staring at us.

We knew immediately we were in trouble: we had insulted them, our Army uniforms mocking symbols of their country's crushing defeat. The crowded courtyard fell silent. Dropping uncounted German bills on the table, we stood up and headed with as much dignified speed as we could muster in the opposite direction of the young men, hoping there was an exit in front of us. We pushed open a heavy door, ran down some steps, and jumped in our car, a dented '49 Opel abandoned by a departing sergeant. We drove, fast, back to the barracks, and changed into our civilian clothes. Then we drove out again to our favorite *biergarten*, 'Der Fliegende Holländer,' where the German bartender liked us—we had our own mugs hanging on the wall—and talked about our near brush with death.

"They would have thrown us over the wall into the river," Murray said. Callow young men exaggerate, but as I remember the incident, my hands get a little cold. He might have been right.

As you'd guess from my name, I'm part German. My grandfather, Harry Christian Meinke, immigrated through Ellis Island toward the end of the 19th Century. He was alone, a young boy from Hannover, about the age of some of the children now trying to cross our own borders. His parents had died, and he was sent by cousins to live with related poor German immigrants, fishermen in Brooklyn, who lived in shacks along Sheepshead Bay. I doubt if they were overjoyed to see young Harry, but they took him in. In my earliest clear memories of Brooklyn, I'm in a creaky old rowboat with Grandpa, breathing the strong smell of fish mixed with his cigar, learning to pull in sheepshead, flounder, and the occasional scary eel.

These boyhood reflections, mingling with those of our American team (with its German coach), bring yet another image to mind: the sonnet engraved on the pedestal of the Statue of Liberty, greater than our or Germany's boasting national anthems. For a century—until just a few years ago—its famous conclusion had spoken to the deep core of American hearts and values:

> ... *"Give me your tired, your poor,*
> *Your huddled masses yearning to breathe free,*
> *The wretched refuse of your teeming shore.*
> *Send these, the homeless, tempest-tost to me,*
> *I lift my lamp beside the golden door."*
>
> –from "The New Colossus" by Emma Lazarus (1849-1887)

SAKARI MOMOI, AGE 111

SEPTEMBER 4, 2014

Poetry & Age

The buffalo eats grass, I eat him, and when I die, the earth eats me and sprouts more grass. Therefore nothing is ever lost, and each thing is everything forever, though all things move.

–Old Lodge Skins, Indian chief in Thomas Berger's novel *Little Big Man* (1964)

The other day I read a brief article in *The New York Times* about the world's oldest man, Sakari Momoi. The Guinness World Records lists him as 111, which caught my eye because that's the exact age of Jack Crabb, the 111-year-old narrator of one of our great American novels, *Little Big Man*, which I'd been thinking about because its author, Thomas Berger, died last month, at 89. 111 is a memorable number, so the least I can do is think a little about this coincidence. As Linda Loman, Willy's wife, cries in *Death of a Salesman*, "Attention must be paid!" (Which makes me remember, in a "six degrees" sort of way, that Dustin Hoffman starred as Jack Crabb in the film adaptations of *Little Big Man* [1970] and Willy Loman in *Death of a Salesman* [1985]). The world, like our brain, is a huge spider web: touch it anywhere and the rest of it shivers.

Sakari Momoi was, until he retired, a life-long educator, and is still a lover and reader of Japanese poetry. This isn't a lot of information about a long sojourn, but one can infer a few things. One, Japanese schools must be a lot less stressful to teach in than American schools, where they're debating whether or not to arm our teachers, whose life expectancy's a lot shorter than Mr. Momoi's.

And two, the fact that he's read poetry all his life may prove that it's good for you, like collard greens. I find this worrisome: the health gurus might take up poetry, and that'll be the end of it. The very fact that no one understands it means that reading a poem stirs the brain's blood in unusual directions, thus oiling the whole contraption. But giving poetry utilitarian values would ring its death knell. I've always liked the idea that poetry's a subversive activity, and was certainly bad for your health, as it's usually consumed and listened to along with bad wine, dubious cheese, and various kinds of smoke in the air.

But, really, why do the Japanese live so long? Masoa Okawa, the oldest living woman at age 116, is also Japanese. (A French woman, Jeanne Calment, lived to be 122, the longest on record, port wine possibly being more restorative than sake.) Americans don't do badly, but have nothing to boast about: the U.S. is only 37th on the longevity list of the world's countries. One clear reason for this is that all of the countries ahead of us—France, Japan, Italy, Spain, Australia, Switzerland *et al.*, have had for decades some form of single payer universal health coverage, as opposed to our system, which was to force the poor to do without, until some disaster sends them staggering to the Emergency Ward. That's our healthcare trifecta: inefficient, costly, and heartless. With the Affordable Care Act, we're changing, but with all its obstacles this will take a long time.

Both Jack Crabb and Sakari Momoi survived through two distinct civilizations, split by major violence: the Battle of Little Big Horn (Custer's Last Stand) in 1876; and Hiroshima and Nagasaki in 1945. Momoi's no showboat, but at 111 he's no doubt aware that the oldest recorded living *man* was—surprise!—his countryman, Jiroeman Kimura, who made it to 116. Momoi told the Guinness people that he'd "like to live another two years." Like Berger's Jack Crabb there seems to be acceptance in his heart and a competitive twinkle in his eye. I think he may be going for the record.

> *Thank you for making me a Human Being! Thank you for helping me become a warrior! Thank you for all my victories and for all my defeats. Thank you for my vision, and for the blindness in which I saw further.*
>
> –from the prayer of Old Lodge Skins at the conclusion of *Little Big Man*, by Thomas Berger (1924-2014)

Editor's Note: Sakori Momoi died on July 5, 2015. An Indonesian man, Mbah Gotho, whose birth certificate says he was born in 1870, has just celebrated his 146th birthday.

JAMES DICKEY

SEPTEMBER 18, 2014

Poets & Scientists Unite

Hermann Helmholtz said the problem facing
the scientist is this:
reduce a creek a kiss
a flaming coal from this random tracing
to some irreducible final text
dancing to the air
of the inverse square
and we are left with the question: what next?

After the past presidential election it was widely noted that President Obama had been elected by a greedy lot of special-interest voters looking for "gifts" from mushy-hearted Democrats. These groups include those made famous by Romney's 2012 quote about "the 47% who will never take personal responsibility for their lives," plus a handful of communist professors who put Obama over the top.

Two other minorities that went heavily for President Obama have been less publicized: scientists and poets.

While numerically small, these men and women create works that in one way or another affect millions (OK, I admit: these days scientists touch more people than poets do—but we'll be sorry). In any case, these days both groups are overwhelmingly Democratic: a Pew poll showed 6% of scientists were Republicans; poets apparently (and typically) refused to be polled, but their Republican number is surely even smaller. Tellingly, in America they both work in the same arena: colleges and universities. Put a dowser over a map of America, set it to find Democrats instead of water, and you'll find the point dipping thirstily over colleges and universities, even in red states like Texas and Georgia.

Our struggling public school system is flawed, particularly not helping those children locked in poverty (of the 35 "developed countries," the U.S. rates next to last in terms of relative child poverty, above only Romania). But our shining beacon in the world of education is the American university system, where the free flow of pure information—polluted elsewhere by advertising and skewed political reporting—makes it about the only forum where truth on any subject has a chance to rise to the top. It's no accident that students from all over the world come here to study and learn, but for Republicans the typical university campus is a no-fly zone.

The Republicans disbelief in climate change (see Governor Scott and Senator Rubio) has been catastrophic for our future, and is the result of their distrust of science in general (vaccinations, fluoridation, etc.) Correspondingly, their party's belief in belligerency as foreign policy, flaring up once again in criticism of President Obama, is dangerous for our present; and is at least partially the result of not listening to poets. Of course, one big reason Republicans like to fight wars and science at the same time is money. Big oil, big NRA, and the big Koch brothers support them; forget about scientists and poets.

Poetry's a minority taste, though many Americans turn to it in times of need. Symbolic of Republican disdain for "pointy-headed intellectuals," only Democratic presidents have had poets read at their inaugurations: Robert Frost at Kennedy's, Maya Angelou and Miller Williams at Clinton's, James Dickey at Carter's, Elizabeth Alexander and Richard Blanco at Obama's, their diverse backgrounds representing the wide embrace of the Democratic party.

Scientists and poets may be dorky human beings like everyone else, but science and poetry instruct the mind and heart of the world, and we should listen to what they tell us.

About today's poem: Our scientific children were surprised I'd even heard of Helmholtz, a German physicist known for his theories on vision and sound (involving the inverse square root, about which I haven't a clue). I was embarrassed to confess what attracted me was his name—a perfect trochaic pentameter line: HERmann LUDwig FERdin ANDvon HELMholtz (which matches the rhythm of King Lear's last exclamation, NEVer NEVer NEVer NEVer NEVer).

But there is always another layer
above beyond below
the last answer: we know
the scientist and poet shape their prayer
with Newton and Frost who searched for order
instead of answers and found
such grace in number and sound
they glorify the spell of light on water

  –both quotes from "Hermann Ludwig Ferdinand
   Von Helmhotz," from *Liquid Paper: New & Selected Poems*
   by Peter Meinke (U. of Pittsburgh Press 1991)

WILLIAM BLAKE

OCTOBER 2, 2014

Feminism & Language

Flower in the crannied wall,
I pluck you out of the crannies,
I hold you here, root and all, in my hand,
Little flower—but if I could understand
What you are, root and all, and all in all,
I should know what God and man is.

   –"Flower in the Crannied Wall"
   by Alfred, Lord Tennyson (1809-1892)

Scientists and poets have always struggled to find the hidden meaning of our world, the secret formula that explains everything. Of course, if they did discover what "God and Man is," as Tennyson said, they'd still have left out Woman, who probably hold the secret. Even Tennyson's Christian God, portrayed as male, may not quite understand.

Decades ago, lost in the miasma of time, I heard a charming exchange of ideas between a man and a woman that went something like this:

Man—"Well, whenever I say *man* or *mankind*, everyone knows that this includes *woman*, too."

Woman—"That's what *you* think."

And there you have it. It doesn't matter if the man was speaking the "truth," that when he said things like "All men are created equal," in his own mind he included women. I suppose that's what our

Founding Fathers would say. (What our Founding Mothers thought hasn't been revealed by the early historians, who were male.)

Of course Tennyson can plead metrical necessity in his poem. He couldn't really fit "I should know what God and man and woman is" into the rhythmical scheme of his lines, not to mention its grammar. Even "I should know what God and people is" doesn't work. In a way, our thought processes get corrupted by our vocabulary, the seemingly inclusive and innocuous word "man" rendering "woman" invisible.

It's a problem of language. Thomas Jefferson, the principle writer of our Declaration of Independence, wrote: "We hold these truths to be self-evident: that all men are created equal . . ." High language indeed, particularly for those days, but it doesn't only omit women: it leaves out America's slaves, at least 15% of the country, as well as the various Indian tribes (i.e. "savages") that we had also defeated or deceived. Today, this omission seems "self-evident," but not so in 1776. They knew that women and slaves and Indians existed, but these didn't register as individuals. James Madison (calling them "other people") proposed each slave be counted in the census as three-fifths of a person, for purposes of official population counts and taxes. Women counted as whole people, but couldn't vote.

Well, language is hard. In our own time, pretty soon it will be "self-evident" that gays deserve equal rights, but this is still evolving. Even the word "gay" didn't grab hold of today's meaning till the 1960's. But it caught on fast: By the seventies I couldn't recite Wordsworth's famous "I Wandered Lonely as A Cloud" to my students without having them snigger at "A poet could not but be gay, / In such a jocund company."

Even what we should call the descendants of our former slaves is complicated and changing. "Negro" got corrupted, "Afro-American" seems illogical, "black" seems incorrect (as, of course, does "white"—and "pale-face" suggests panic). "People of color" is unwieldy, and implies that others are "people without color," which is untrue.

Still, we should listen to the poets. Fifty years before Tennyson, the visionary William Blake saw that the old way of looking at things was killing our society. To "see" clearly we need to develop the right words. This is a slow process.

Problem: of course, I'm a man, and probably don't know what I'm talking about. All my life I've tried to exhibit the "manly" virtues, primarily physical ones like strength or courage ("weakling," for example, is a seemingly neutral adjective, that in actual use applies only to boys or men). This means that, like our athletic President Gerald Ford, I probably played "too much football without a helmet."

> *The Harlots cry from Street to Street*
> *Shall weave Old Englands winding Sheet ...*
> *We are led to Believe a Lie*
> *When we see not Thro the Eye*
>
>   –from "Auguries of Innocence"
>   by William Blake (1757-1827)

CHARLIE CRIST

OCTOBER 16, 2014

Flip-flops

Tomorrow if it come
I (if I'm around)
will barricade our home
from the hullabalooing town
corking the walls of my room
unless I decide to go out...

"Friends and foes ask: Is Charlie Crist for real?" This question kicked off the Tampa Bay Times titillating tell-all article, "Knowing Charlie." Of course, only his foes ask this, a natural segue into an attack on his metamorphosis from creeping devouring Republican caterpillar to a fluttering nectar-sipping Democrat butterfly. The thrust of the TBT piece was that Crist will say anything to get elected. Like Captain Renault, we were shocked, shocked...

But no one knows what's inside Crist, or any politician—or even any person. He really seemed to grow uncomfortable as Republicans hardened their stances on all fronts. A born moderate, Crist wants everyone to like him, even the poor. He naturally flowed into the old Republican party, like the younger Mitt Romney, who brought Romneycare to Massachusetts before metamorphosing in reverse to Romney the Disdainer of Lazy Whiners.

As to flips, the Tea Party-driven GOP has veered so far right even President Reagan wouldn't recognize it. If you doubt this, google Reagan on "health care," "assault rifles," "taxes," "immigration reform" or "climate change."

Crist, the opposite of Governor Scott, is Mr. Accessible. We've seen him in our Publix on the South Side, or walking by Midtown Sundries talking animatedly with two companions, or chatting quietly with a friend at the Oyster Bar. He seems to be everywhere at once. The thought occurs, there are smiling doubles involved, nodding their heads and taking any hand that comes within shaking distance. How else fight the avalanche of Scott's TV attacks?

This election should be about specific policies, getting the right ones enacted. Forget the Why, or even the Who, and concentrate on the What. The Tampa Bay Times is generally clear on this (i.e. "Scott gets an F on Education," etc.) but Adam Smith's "balanced" discussion replayed Republican ads like "Crist represents everything you hate about politics," whereas what we're really against is ideological rigidity resulting in policies that harm us: against minimum wage, equal pay, affordable health care, environmental control. As for the economy, Scott's trumpeted "strength," Tampa Bay and Miami rank the lowest in median household income of all comparable cities *in the country*. Water's lapping at our eroding shoreline.

Many believe Crist has done the right thing for the wrong reason—like a child getting a good report card for money—so instead of gaining credit for changing his stance on, say, gay marriage, he gets attacked for it. But instead of focusing on murky "motives," we have to decide who'll cast the votes on education, women's rights, immigration, and climate change to move Florida forward before we become a stock joke, as real and metaphorical waters rise around us. Think of it this way: President Obama has steered us through precarious waters toward becoming a smarter and more tolerant country. Who—Rick Scott or Charlie Crist—is better suited to helping our state follow that direction?

When I was a boy we'd lie down on the living room rug to listen to "The Shadow" on the radio. "*Who knows what evil lurks in the hearts of men?"* the deep voice would announce, as I'd peer guiltily around at my sisters, wondering if they had an idea. But only the Shadow seemed to know, and we learned we should leave that up to him.

At the end of the show, the God-like voice (Orson Welles' was the first) affirmed that *"The weed of crime bears bitter fruit."* So far Scott, supported by the Koch Brothers and Duke Energy, has already bought our state once, and has escaped tasting that fruit. It's about time that he does, and it's up to Florida voters to see that he swallows it.

>*I suffer gladly*
>*This foolish uncertainty*
>*For which we've found no cure*
>*I'm confused therefore I'm alive:*
> Still lie the dead sure

>   –both quotes from "Certitude," by Peter Meinke
>   (in *Zinc Fingers*, U. of Pittsburgh Press, 2000)

DANNIE ABSE

OCTOBER 30, 2014

The Good Doctor

White coat and purple coat
  a sleeve from both he sews.
That white is always stained with blood,
  that purple by the rose.

In a popular conception, a poet is someone who not only writes murkily, slouching in a garret, but often emerges as some combination of alcoholic suicidal bottom-pincher. But just as our poems are misread, so are our lives; and the closer you look at the lives of most poets, the more they look like everyone else's.

These thoughts burbled up because of the recent death of Dannie Abse, a long-time friend, and the most decorated Welsh poet since Dylan Thomas. The thing about Dannie was that, except for being a marvelous poet, he was a good guy in the normal way.

In the fall of 1984, we were in London, where I was teaching a course on Contemporary English Poetry, and invited Dr. Abse to read to our class. I'd heard about Dannie, a Welsh writer living in London, because he was also a practicing doctor who often read to medical students in America, including those at USF. With a small budget to invite poets to talk, I called Dannie and discovered he lived nearby in Golders Green, seven stops up from Goodge Street (our nearest tube station; we loved the name).

He was a hit as soon as he walked in the door. Good-looking and sturdy, with an unruly shock of white hair, he connected easily with the students. His poems and stories made them laugh and cry; one poem, "In the Theatre," in which a patient undergoing a brain operation suddenly begins howling "Leave my soul alone" over and over, actually made them gasp.

Our real friendship with Dannie and his wife Joan began a few nights later, when we met at his favorite restaurant, the "Great Nepalese," a gem stuck in the middle of a dingy London street near Euston Station. We talked for hours over Chicken Kashmiri and Lamb Tikka, and many glasses of wine. He was erudite, funny, generous, and a great sports fan, particularly of his beloved Cardiff Bluebirds, the Welsh soccer team.

In the years to come, we had many more memorable meetings. He looked at the world with fond skepticism, and liked the things that we all liked. Once, when Dannie was reading at Eckerd, two other distinguished poets, William Jay Smith and William Meredith, came to listen. When we offered to take them out to lunch (courtesy of Eckerd!), these sophisticated bards put their heads together and decided they just wanted a good pizza. We have a fine photo of them in front of Vito & Michael's Pizzeria, near the old Beach Theater.

We last saw Joan and Dannie in 2002, when we were visiting London with our colleague, Ken Keeton, and his wife Cece. Spontaneously, the Abses invited all of us over for what turned out to be a 3-course lunch, complete with wine, tea, and coffee in their garden. Then they drove us to nearby Hampstead Heath, the beautiful park where John Keats walked and wrote before he went off to Italy to die. We wandered along the pathways, winding up at Kenwood House and Museum, where Joan, a prominent art historian, told us, among many other things, that the marvelous Rembrandt painting there was "the most popular self-portrait in England."

In 2005, in a tragedy still hard to grasp, a driver ran a stop sign and crashed into their car, killing Joan instantly. Much of his writing after that, completely without self-pity, has to do with loss and loneliness, interspersed with tales of their happy marriage. He had children and many friends, but continued to live in their lovely house, alone, working on his poems till the day he died.

And phantom rose and blood most real
  compose a hybrid style;
white coat and purple coat
  few men can reconcile.

White coat and purple coat
  can each be worn in turn
but in the white a man will freeze
  and in the purple burn.

—"White Coat, Purple Coat" is from *New Selected Poems* by Dannie Abse (1923-2014), Sheep Meadow Press, NY, 2012

Like me on **Facebook!**

NOVEMBER 13, 2014

ISIS Crisis

Hark, how the peoples surge and sigh,
And laughters fail, and greetings die.

Statisticians assure us that the world's getting safer. We live longer, crime is down, wars less frequent, diets healthier. But why don't we feel better? Why so fearful?

Mark Twain liked to say there are three kinds of lies: lies, damned lies, and statistics. This is particularly true in America, where our political system, fueled by an irresponsible media, pours out all three of those like a BP oil rig in the Gulf. Health care, gun control, Social Security—everything becomes politicized and terrifying: *Death panels! Murder! Bankruptcy!* We live life in italics, with exclamation points.

Let's take the two most recent terrors, Ebola and ISIS. Although at this moment only one person, Thomas Eric Duncan—a Liberian—has died here from Ebola, our country seems gripped by an unshakeable fear, as politicians seek to blame Obama for letting it run amok over our borders.

Suddenly this grisly disease is in our midst, and we're panting like the trapped party-goers in "The Masque of the Red Death," as if "Darkness and Decay and the Red Death held illimitable dominion over all." Here in town, USF St Pete has canceled a visit by 12 African journalists—none even from infected countries—who were here, ironically, as part of the Edward R. Murrow Visiting Journalists' program. Standing up against Senator Joe McCarthy, Murrow famously said, "No one can terrify a whole nation unless we are all his accomplices." He would have applauded a neighbor of ours who promptly held a laughter-filled dinner party for all of the visiting journalists. (Back then we had Murrow; now we have CNN's hysterical Wolf Blitzer, nominated by Andy Borowitz for "the person most Americans favor quarantining.")

ISIS is the other crisis. Like Ebola, they're a true scourge, but they're not about to overrun America, either. ISIS (the "Islamic State") is a hyper-inflated splinter group blending a reactionary religion with medieval violence and slick videos to recruit unhappy youngsters to inflict brutal damage in Iraq and Syria. They use certain mosques, along with Facebook and other media ads, to appeal to uneducated young men (and a few young women) who feel lost and inadequate in Western society with its freedoms and excesses.

It's true that they've touched a weakness in us. A small percentage but numerically high number of Americans have been ignored (by family, by media, by government) to implode upon themselves or explode upon others. For example, we have the best Army in the world, hands down; we spend more on military might than most of our friends and enemies put together. But we're not taking good enough care of the most vulnerable of us in our society in general—and even in our Army. The number of military veteran suicides—22 per day—is going up, as is the number of military rapes—70 per day. These are staggering numbers and, even given the dubious accuracy of statistics, they reveal in America's underbelly a multitude of men and women who need help, and respond to radical calls to religious glory.

We should turn down the noise blaring from our radios and tv sets. ISIS and Ebola are real threats, but we have worse ones: climate change, drunk driving, drug wars, watered-down education, street crime, cancer, cigarettes, poverty, and the NRA. ISIS and Ebola are real, but they're not threats to America. Let's just deal with them, and work on the true problems facing us.

When I was a boy in Brooklyn attending the Lutheran Church, our minister once read to us from *Revelations* about the Four Horsemen of the Apocalypse. On their vivid horses—white, red, black, and pale—they represented, he told us, false prophets, war, famine, and death; and they were galloping after us. Now, that was scary!

> *...And such are we—*
> *Unreasoning, sanguine, visionary—*
> *That I can hope*
> *Health, love, friends, scope*
> *In full for thee; can dream thou'lt find*
> *Joys seldom yet attained by humankind!*
>
> –both quotes from "To An Unborn Pauper Child" by Thomas Hardy (1840-1928)

JIMMY CARTER

NOVEMBER 27, 2014

Walking the Walk

Dear Lord of all the fields
What am I going to do?
Street lights, blue-force and frail
As the homes of men, tell me how to do it...

Let's cut Jimmy Carter a break. I'm thinking about him because 1) he recently turned 90 and is still out there doing good deeds. 2) We just saw the movie "Killing the Messenger," a story about Gary Webb, the Phoenix Mercury journalist who stumbled on the truth of what turned out to be the Iran/Contra scandal. This sleazy operation began in the Ronald Reagan era, with Oliver North and Elliott Abrams flitting like bats around it. Who knows if President Reagan knew about it, or understood the terrible things—including Contra death squads and massive drug trafficking—that happened; but my first thought was that this would never have happened under President Carter.

And 3), the midterm Democratic debacle was similar to the crushing of Carter by Reagan. People in the know (e.g.; Nate Silver, though he missed on the Scott vs. Crist cliffhanger) saw it coming for a long time, reminding us of 1980 when the Republicans first nominated a handsome mediocre actor named Ronald Reagan. "An *actor?*" we said. "Are you serious?" A friend of ours, Faye Joyce, the first female Political Editor of the *St. Petersburg Times*, shook her head. "Just wait a few minutes," Faye said. "You're going to be real surprised." Faye didn't think much of Reagan: she was skeptical of the American voters. Carter was the victim of bad timing (the failed Iranian hostage rescue attempt) and bad luck (a weak economy), neither his fault. Also, Reagan had a better voice and a (somewhat canned} sense of humor

Carter won his election in 1976 because he was a committed Christian instead of a committed felon. He'd been a decent Governor of Georgia, the country was sick over Watergate, and his preachy religiosity pulled in a lot of voters the Democrats would eventually lose to a prejudiced Tea Party. To an upset country, his opponent, President Ford, was the incumbent who pardoned the disgraced President Nixon.

Carter actually did fine as a president, returning Panama to its rightful owners, and getting closer to a Middle East peace than anyone else, with the 1978 Camp David Accords (still in effect today), signed by Egyptian President Anwar Sadat and Israeli Prime Minister Menachem Begin. In all accounts, although Sadat and Begin went on to be awarded the Nobel Peace Prize, it was Carter's gentle but unrelenting persistence that got those two lifelong antagonists together.

But in his post-Presidency years, Carter has come into his own (and his own Nobel Peace Prize in 2002). After leaving their presidencies, Nixon returned to politics, Ford played golf, Reagan admired his Library, Bush I beams at his progenies' political success, Clinton alternates between doing good and doing well, and Bush II churns out oil paintings. But Jimmy Carter has walked the walk of a good Christian, working tirelessly to help humankind, especially the poor and oppressed. Through the Carter Center, he's nearly eliminated river blindness from Africa and elsewhere, delivering over 200 million doses of Mectizan (donated by Merck Pharmaceutical). He's monitored 90+ elections in shaky countries, and travels the world promoting democracy and waging peace. Somehow, he (and Rosalynn with him) still find time to help build houses with Habitats for Humanity, and teach Sunday school in his home town of Plains, Georgia. He often speaks truth to power, irritating many misbehaving governments, including Israel and America.

Both idealistic and practical, Jimmy Carter's trying to make the world a safer and healthier place. He not only chose James Dickey to write an inaugural poem, but has taken the poem to heart, and is living it. Happy Thanksgiving, Jimmy!

> *... More kindness, dear Lord*
> *Of the renewing green. That is where it all has to start:*
> *With the simplest things. More kindness will do nothing less*
> *Than save every sleeping one*
> *And night-walking one*
> *Of us.*
> *My life belongs to the world. I will do what I can.*
>
> –from "The Strength of Fields," by James Dickey (1923-1997), composed for and read at President Carter's Inaugural Ball, Jan. 20, 1977

GRAMOPHONE

DECEMBER 10, 2014

Confidence

I too awaited the expected guest.
He, the young man carbuncular, arrives,
A small house agent's clerk, with one bold stare,
One of the low on whom assurance sits
As a silk hat on a Bradford millionaire . . .

When I was in high school, I played on the baseball team, and one shadowless spring day we were playing our rival, Boonton High, which fielded a very large pitcher on the mound who was being watched by major league scouts. In the first inning I surprised everybody by knocking a clean single to left and, feeling cocky about my hit, took a long lead off first base. The pitcher tried to pick me off but I slid back safely. Brushing myself off, I heard my girl friend's voice rise from the sparsely filled grandstand: "You'll never get *him*!"

I of course took an even more daring lead on the next pitch; and was promptly picked off, never to get on base again during a long afternoon.

Overconfidence is characteristic of the American male, and I'm fairly confident—perhaps overconfident—that this holds true for males across the globe. Personality tests indicate that this is often matched by *under*confidence on the part of most females.

But as we look at cold statistics, this situation seems backwards. Today, girls outscore boys in school grades in every subject, even math and science, and you'd guess this would bolster their egos. The girls must think, *These idiots not only don't know the capital of Idaho, they can't even add! And they wear baggy shorts.* In addition, if I remember what's now called "middle school" accurately, the girls at that formative age usually grow faster than the boys. I recall dancing at an 8th-grade prom with a partner a head taller than I, and wondering if I should try resting my head on her slender bosom, see what happens. She might kill me, I thought, but still . . .

Many of our most confident male leaders—listen to our so-called primary "debates"— are pretty clearly nincompoops, proud because they don't read anything: not books, not magazines, not scientific articles, certainly not poetry. They lift their biased "info" from the Internet, from emails, from Lewis Carroll (well, I made that up: I'm thinking of Tweedledee and Tweedledum). Whether they're talking about sex ("Rape doesn't cause pregnancy," Congressman Todd Akin); science, ("Science is one of the Four Corners of Deceit"), pundit Rush Limbaugh; climate change ("Climate change is good for your health," Heartland Institute 'think tank'); Iraq ("My belief is we will, in fact, be greeted as liberators," Vice President Dick Cheney) etc., they are all—like me playing baseball—wildly off-base. My favorite remains, oddly enough, one by an overconfident woman, Sarah Palin (the exception that proves the rule): "Refudiate, misunderestimate, wee-wee'd up: English is a living language!" she pouted to Sean Hannity. In subject after subject Americans students show more confidence and less competence than their European and Asian counterparts

T. S. Eliot's "The Waste Land," less influential than it used to be, still can hypnotize us with its rhythmical visions of a decadent society ("I think we are in rat's alley / where the dead man lost their bones"). One of the most disturbing is that overconfident clerk "seducing" an already defeated young woman. Since 1919, when Eliot was writing the "The Waste Land" and American women didn't even have the vote, our society has improved—think Michelle Obama, Janet Yellen, Elizabeth Warren, Hillary Clinton, Elena Kagan, Sonia Sotomayor,

Rachel Maddow—but we still have a long way to go: on the radio as I write this, reporters are debating how many college students are the victims of rape (intolerable, whatever the real percentage). Human change, including the distribution of confidence as well as money, is evolutionary rather than revolutionary.

Of course, many Tea-Partyers still don't believe in evolution, which is a bit of a drag on progress.

> *When lovely woman stoops to folly and*
> *Paces about her room again, alone,*
> *She smoothes her hair with automatic hand,*
> *And puts a record on the gramophone . . .*

–both quotes from "The Waste Land" by T.S. Eliot (1888-1965)

CAROUSEL

DECEMBER 25, 2014

Carousel Christmas

Carnivals and cotton candy
Carousels and calliopes
Fortune-tellers in glass cases
We will always remember these ...

This December Jeanne and I decided to use her drawing of a carousel horse for our annual Christmas card, which is somewhat of an odd choice. We've often been drawn to carousels in romantic places, like the *Jardin du Luxembourg* in Paris, even after our children were grown. With students, we generally stayed at the Hôtel de la Sorbonne, next to the University and near the Luxembourg Gardens. We loved to sit there, with a glass of wine, and watch other people's children waving from the vintage carousel, or sailing their toy boats in the Medici Fountain.

But our earliest carousel, and the most emotional, was the ancient Cafesjians Carousel at the Como Park Zoo in St. Paul. We lived in Minnesota for five years, 1961-65, while I was teaching at Hamline University. By 1965, our four children, Perrie, Peter, Gretchen and Timothy, were ages 6, 5, 3, and 2. We had zero bucks, and Como Park was a common, and free, destination, complete with a lake and a zoo. One day, we put Perrie and Pete on the carousel for the first time; when the music stopped, and they jumped happily off the platform, I looked over at Jeanne, holding the baby carriage with the two youngest: tears were streaming down her cheeks. Seeing them bobbing on their horses, she'd seen the future galloping, carrying the children away.

In any park we visited, when the kids heard the tinny notes of a carousel through trees or around buildings, their ears would prick up like a pony's, and off we'd go. Another word for carousel is "merry-go-round," but the usual music often seems more spooky than merry to us. By now we've seen enough movies set in carnivals, where the thin carousel tunes seem to be saying, *Watch out, don't buy that ticket!*

Once in a while, coming back from a long trip, waiting for our luggage, having visited our children overseas, we'd look at the conveyor belt as the various bags wobbled by, and have more or less the same thought: "You know, this is a carousel, too, except it brings things home." Language is funny.

My favorite Broadway musical (and I love Broadway musicals) is "Carousel," the story of Bill, the doomed carnival barker, and Julie, his working-girl lover. It was the second Rodgers and Hammerstein collaboration, after "Oklahoma," though we first saw it in the 1950's as a movie starring Gordon MacRae and Shirley Jones. The hit song was "You'll Never Walk Alone," but the one Jeanne and I liked best—maybe foreseeing all our kids—was the long "Soliloquy" that Bill sings after learning that Julie is pregnant, imagining the great future of his son or daughter. We'd often semi-sing (like Bill), looking at our newborn children, "but he" (or she) "wouldn't be president if he didn't wanna be."

What about our Christmas card? Well, Christmas has always been about children (by extension from the Child). Carousels are like music boxes, magical Christmas presents that outgrew their box, as in a fairy tale. They were once wild unrideable horses, I'd tell the children, but the princess loved them so much she asked the magician to let her ride them, promising him her jewelry, except for her gold ring, if he could do so. So he charmed the horses into the first carousel and hung her gold ring on a pole near the spinning ride; and the princess rode and rode, as her hair turned from red to grey, leaning to catch the gold ring as she whirled by, but it was always just out of reach.

Well, that wasn't the only ending, of course, because there were many children and many horses; and language is funny. Merry Christmas to all, young and old.

> *Merry-go-rounds quickly turning*
> *Quickly turning for you and me*
> *And the whole world madly turning*
> *Turning, turning 'till you can't see...*

–both quotes from "Carousel" by Jacques Brel (1929-1978)

2015

PIOTR SOMMER

JANUARY 15, 2015

Polish Lessons

Tomorrow is Thursday.
If the world meets its obligations
the following day will be Friday...

When we lived in Poland during 1978-79, its citizens were still under Russian control. Nothing worked. Everyone, except the Communist leaders, was underpaid, resulting in massive inequality. Bribes, fraud, and corruption were normal. No one believed the papers. No one believed anything, even what day it was. Would the *supersam* (supermarket) be open today? If it was, would there be any bananas? Or sugar? No one had the slightest idea.

But when I look back on that year, I feel twinges of optimism, because it felt remarkably like America today. If a divided Poland can recover from such dire straits, why shouldn't a divided America?

Poland not only survived, but is now one of Europe's shining stars. While other countries, East and West, are faltering economically, Poland is slowly but steadily building a strong middle class. It happened fast:

In 1978, in Warsaw, we heard vague rumors of unrest in the shipyards of Gdansk, on the Baltic Coast. In 1979, people whispered that a shipyard electrician named Lech Wałesa was leading a revolutionary movement, but no one seemed sure. Back home in 1980, we received a large red and white poster from a Polish friend, *SOLIDARNOSC*: the revolutionary union, Solidarity, had been formed. In 1989 Solidarity supporters won every seat available in the Polish parliament, the first falling domino in the Communist collapse, electing Wałesa president of Poland in 1990. By 2004 Poland had joined the European Union, where it's flourishing.

How did Poland do it, and what can we learn from them? First of all, the Poles were non-violent. They, as much as any people, have seen what violence does. Poland, defenseless on the flat North European Plain, has been invaded by Russia, Germany, Sweden, Austria, Turkey, and Hungary. In my poetry class, they loved Emily Dickinson's lines *Success is counted sweetest / By those who ne'er succeed. / To comprehend a nectar / Requires sorest need.* "We understand suffering," one student said. "It glues us together."

To us, at first, Poland seemed defeated. But underneath the rubble, they were joining hands. A solidly Catholic country, their Catholicism seems more familial and political than religious. At a party I asked why so many of the crosses on top of the churches were lit up at night. We thought it might mean, in a Communist country, *Jesus lives.* "It means," our host said, "that Poland is still fighting." When Karol Woytyla (a published poet, among other things) was elected Pope John Paul II, a million people, including us, surged into Victory Square when he visited Warsaw in 1979, while government soldiers lined up in the side streets, nervously clutching their rifles. But the masses didn't riot.

The Poles seemed dignified, generous, kind to each other and to guests. Piotr Sommer, the fine poet quoted today, and his wife Jola, helped us navigate Warsaw's potholes in innumerable ways. The only businesses that seemed to flourish in those days were the *kwiaty* (flower) stores. We were often invited to dinner and other parties, and everyone brought flowers. The dinners were mostly simple, and included good bread and good vodka—two items in abundance. Their apartments were small, as was ours ("Gee," our teen-age daughter said when we arrived, "I feel like Anne Frank.")

If we want to regain our country's soul, we need to be patient and civil, like the Poles. Never give in to despair. Keep a sense of humor (the Poles were mordantly funny) and hang in there, waiting for the right man or woman to lead us.

I'll end with their typical New Year's Eve toast (translated to today): Raising vodka glasses, they'd smile and say, "May 2015 be worse than 2016!" They could laugh because they knew they were in it for the long haul. *Na zdrowie.*

If it doesn't, it could even be Sunday,
and no one will ever guess
where our life got mislaid.

–from "Days of the week" by Piotr Sommer (*Things to Translate and other poems*, Bloodaxe Books, Great Britain 1991)

PETER MEINKE

HAWAII

JANUARY 22, 2015

Hawaiian Sigh

I Kaka'ako mAkou
'Al ana I ka pipi stew
He mea ma'a mau ia
   For you and I

That ungrammatical "For you and I" always grated when we heard Israel Kamakawiwa'ole (sensibly called "Iz" in Hawaii) sing it repeatedly in one of his hit songs. But that guy could sing. When we first saw him, in a huge auditorium in Honolulu, he had to be forklifted onto the stage while the crowd cheered as if the machine were hoisting Michelangelo's 'David' to the podium. At his biggest, Iz weighed in at 767 pounds, but the tones that flowed out of that body were sheer gold. Literally, he was a Hawaiian treasure.

In 1993, on turning 60, I retired from Eckerd College. We had no debts, but it was a huge cut in pay, and I told Jeanne she was brave, taking a chance that we could survive on a much-reduced budget to concentrate on writing and drawing. Out of a truly blue sky, while we were figuring out how to do this, the telephone rang, and a pleasant voice asked if I'd be interested in being writer-in-residence for the fall semester at the University of Hawaii. Steadying myself against the dining room wall, I took a deep breath and said as casually as I could manage, "Sounds good."

This changed our lives, setting a pattern for the next 20 years: an "adventure" at some college or university for a semester, a light teaching load, and no committees. But Hawaii set a very high bar. Last month, we returned for the first time, as our son Tim and his wife Aya had just bought a house in Kailua, and invited us for Christmas. I'm happy to report that Hawaii is still magical.

One would think Hawaii wouldn't be especially attractive to Floridians, just more of the same: sunshine, palm trees, beaches. But the first impression of Hawaii is of its dramatic volcanic mountains, like a scene from a Disney fairy tale, except that they're real. In Kailua, the mountains were right in our back yard, and the beaches practically in the front. While we were there, President Obama was vacationing just a short walk away. One afternoon his cavalcade, probably heading toward the golf course, passed by in front of Pinky's, our neighborhood pupu bar; and the crowd, including us, waved and shouted Happy New Year—Hawaii's a very Democratic state, and loves its native son.

Visually, Hawaii's a South Pacific equivalent of Paris. From almost every corner there's something interesting to look at: the omnipresent mountains, magnificent spreading monkeypad trees, white sand beaches with cool multi-colored waters, exotic flowers and birds—small Red-Crested Cardinals, with scarlet heads and white-scarfed necks fluttered around our street. Because of sensible building restrictions it's not overbuilt or overpopulated (plus, obviously, it's expensive to get there).

For my birthday, we decided to go to Buzz's, a steakhouse the newspaper—the lively Star-Advertiser—claimed was Obama's favorite restaurant. Jeanne asked the waitress what Obama usually ordered. "Teriyaki steak" she told us. "A *very* good choice!" That evening, we all drank and ate like kings, or at least presidents.

Hawaii's a paradise. Still, given the chance, would we move there from St. Pete? It's lovely to breathe clear air below its star-crowded sky—*there's Orion's belt!*—and reassuring to have a Democratic governor and legislature. But we wouldn't be completely happy without the arts scene here, the theatres, galleries, movies, colleges, libraries and restaurants clustered together near us. We can see why our president goes there—you feel better, you breathe deeper, you smile more: people just seem nicer. You can rest. Once in a while, a Hawaii-fix would be good for us all.

Israel's most famous hit is a soulful version of "Somewhere over the Rainbow" (Hawaii has frequent rainbows, often double ones) melting into "What a Wonderful World." It catches the mood of this state, whose often fierce football team is called "The Rainbows"— and no one teases them about it.

When Israel died the Hawaiian flag flew at half-mast.

To Kaka'ako we go
Eating beef stew
Always a good time
    For you and I

  –Lyrics from "Henehene Kou 'Aka'" by Israel Kamakawiwo'ole (1959-1997)

ARCHIE BUNKER

FEBRUARY 5, 2015

Racism & Kramer

after the murder,
after the burial
Emmett's mother is a pretty-faced thing;
the tint of pulled taffy.
She sits in a red room,
drinking black coffee . . .

The continuing backlash to the riots in Ferguson sent me back to some old thoughts about racism in America. Sixty years ago, in 1955, a fourteen-year-old black boy named Emmett Till was tortured, murdered, and dumped in the Tallahatchie River outside of Sumner, Mississippi. He had (maybe) flirted with or whistled at a white woman. (At 14!) Photos of his battered body became a symbol of the hatred smoldering in the hearts of American Southerners and others.

In recent months we've seen appalling photos of the beheading of two American journalists and others by the ISIS terrorists. Just as Emmitt's murder helped bring about a change in America's attitude toward racism (and the passing of the Civil Rights Act of 1957), so the executions of Steven Sotloff and James Foley have triggered a turning point in our "war" against terror.

Racists and terrorists display similar traits: cruelty to the weak and defenseless, a perversion of religious beliefs, blind certainty that they're right, and rage based on the fear—or even the knowledge—that they're on the losing side.

But a "manifesto" I received makes me wonder if America has changed enough. It's called "Proud to Be White," and like many similar screeds, it's mean-minded and untrue in both content and attribution. This one claims to have been spoken by Michael Richards ("Kramer" in the Seinfeld comedy show), while defending some racist remarks he made in one of his stand-up routines. Richards had been criticized for using the "n-word," and he apologized for this on the Letterman show, saying, "For me to be at a comedy club and flip out and say this crap, I'm deeply, deeply, sorry." Now he has another burden: racists, grasping on to his remarks made in anger at some hecklers, have falsely attached his name to "Proud to Be White," and are sending it around the Internet.

Back in the seventies and eighties, another famous comedian, Carroll O'Connor, played the part of Archie Bunker, a blue-collar bigot who despised blacks, gays, feminists, almost anyone different, including his liberal son-in-law Michael Stivic (played by Rob Reiner), whom he usually addressed by "Hey Meat-head, you dumb Polack." Audiences laughed at Archie's bigotry, which was only skin-deep: in the shows, he usually changed his mind when confronted with the actual person he'd been insulting.

The racism of "Proud to Be White" runs deeper. It's as if Archie Bunker has come back without a sense of humor. It begins, "You pass me on the street and sneer in my direction. You call me 'White boy,' 'Cracker,' 'Honkey,' 'Whitey,' 'Caveman' and that's OK. But when I call you Nigger, Kike, Towel head, Sand-nigger, Camel Jocky, Beaner, Gook, or Chink … you call me a racist."

Oh, the horror!

You can easily find "Proud to Be White" on the Internet. The real problem is that in 2014 America, this rant is pulled from the same dark lava behind Governor Romney's speech about the 47% of "takers," behind the effort by Florida and other states with Republican governors to limit the vote, behind the lack of civility toward President Obama, and behind the hatred of "Obamacare" (which, after all, though one can disagree with it, is mainly an effort to give health insurance to the poor among us).

In 1956 William Faulkner, responding to Emmett Till's murder, observed that "the fourteen-year-old boy not only refuses to be frightened, but, unarmed, alone in the dark, so frightens the two armed adults that they must destroy him . . . What are we Mississippians afraid of?"

The question can still be asked. What are the people who are circulating "Proud to Be White" afraid of?

> *She kisses her killed boy*
>   *and she is sorry.*
> *Chaos in windy grays*
>   *through a red prairie.*

> –both quotes from "The Last Quatrain of the Ballad of Emmett Till" by Gwendolyn Brooks (Harper & Row, 1963)

HILLARY CLINTON

FEBRUARY 19, 2015

Ready for Hillary?

A fox knows many things, but the hedgehog knows one big thing.
   —Archilochus (680-645 BC)

I admit I haven't read Hillary Clinton's memoir, *Hard Choices*. It sounds like a boring reference book, but she was fine on the Jon Stewart show: quick, funny, likable. The question these days is, Would we welcome a Clinton run for the presidency? That's like asking, Would we like azaleas to bloom in the spring? It's going to happen whether we welcome it or not.

So it's OK by me, but just like when our azaleas open the oak pollen that makes us sneeze starts to fall, when Hillary-season arrives a miasma of venom will sift down from the Republican cloud like Agent Orange, sticking to everything, so we'll all need extra showers, with an occasional martini, to calm us down.

On the tricky point of what to call her, I prefer "Clinton" instead of "Hillary," except when it might be confusing. Politics is murkier than poetry, but it's off-putting to hear students refer to Emily Dickinson as "Emily," while never calling Robert Frost "Robert." Equal respect and dignity should be up there with equal pay.

Clinton has reached the level of fame where she's often referred to by her initials HRC, like the mother ALP and father HCE in James Joyce's surreal novel *Finnegan's Wake*. Well, her life is only going to get *more* surreal. The radio and TV parrots immediately picked up Karl Rove's inference that she's got something wrong with her head.

But maybe this is a foreshadowing: our actual presidents known by their triple initials—FDR, JFK, and LBJ—were all Democrats. On the other hand, no Democrat has been elected after another since James Buchanan, born in 1791, followed Franklin Pierce.

Seven years after she lost the Democratic primary, Clinton's weaknesses then look like advantages today. In 2008 the major difference between her and Barack Obama was that she was more hawkish, having voted twice to support George Bush and his Iraq War (two *trillion* dollars and counting). This won't have the negative drag it had back then. Using the old Greek poet's analogy (above), Clinton seems like the fox, very good at lots of things, grabbing them as they come by: she's moved smoothly from First Lady to Senator to Secretary of State, and her speeches are astounding for their organization of countless facts. She's ready.

On the other hand, Obama seemed like the more grounded hedgehog, with one overwhelming idea: he could change the country. He's accomplished major changes already—health care, gay rights, economic recovery—but there's a widespread feeling that his dislike of the mundane details of the presidency, like schmoozing and constantly advertising his programs, which Clinton is great at, has held him back.

Clinton's other main drawback was her underestimating Obama—a flaw she's learned from. She's still a confidant candidate, but will never again be an over-confidant one, even if the Republicans nominate Donald Trump. True, only with sinking hearts can we contemplate living through two years of nonstop hysterical attacks: *Benghazi! Monica! Brain damage! Death panels!* But keep that last Republican primary in mind and make no mistake: *that's still the real Republican party.* Perry, Palin, Ryan, Jindal, Bachman, Rubio, Santorum, Gingrich, Paul, Limbaugh, Cruz, McConnell, Rove are its spokespersons, and the Koch brothers are its owners. It will probably try to sneak in a semi-responsible person like Jeb Bush; but this is a runaway party, and already Bush is disclaiming man-influenced climate change. He's no scientist.

For a couple of centuries we've had male presidents with male vice-presidents, with mixed results. Want a real change? How about a Hillary Clinton / Elizabeth Warren ticket?—then at least we'd be assured of having the right debate.

> *Warp and weft, the world is so divided: half is sleeping*
> *While the other half's awake; half—at most—are capable*
> *Of love, and more than half dead at heart. Half are hedgehogs,*
> *the other, foxes . . .*
> *What do you think you are?*
>
> –from "The Banquet of Donny and Ari," by Naomi Guttman, published by Brick Books, Ontario, Canada (2014) .

PHILIP LEVINE

MARCH 5, 2015

The Liberal Arts

*Some things
you know all your life. They are so simple and true
they must be said without elegance, meter and rhyme,
they must be laid on the table beside the salt shaker,
the glass of water . . .*

The liberal arts have often been under the gun, but more so in recent times, when the word "liberal" means "creep" to half our country. Democrats, who generally embrace the liberal values, are afraid to use the word. And because it's been so poorly defended, the liberal arts foundation that made our education the envy of the world is in danger of collapsing.

Cuts in funding are being made from kindergarten through the universities; and when the schools have to decide what to cut, they're looking at the liberal arts, mainly literature, history, poetry, art, music. When they add something, it's usually work-and-career related.

What Samuel Johnson said about poetry is true about "liberal": "Why Sir, it is much easier to say what it is not." Liberalism isn't restrictive, closed, suppressive, stingy. Imagine a funnel. Liberal education is an open-ended funnel which provides a wide *general* basis for its recipients to become free citizens in a democracy. The "work-based" changes being inflicted upon schools reverse the funnel, pouring "practical" information out of the little end to mold narrowly-based engineers, lawyers, professionals and semi-professionals. Even my beloved slow-to-change *alma mater*, Hamilton College, is paying "heightened attention to career preparation."

When I went there, in the 1950's, it offered the traditional liberal education combining science and the arts. Being taught broadly to be skeptical in a polite way, most students developed a nose for false statement. In our day, we were required to take four years of public speaking, a much-derided but ultimately useful course run by a deep-voiced professor we called Swampy Marsh. Debate, memorized speeches and poems, and—most terrifying—impromptu: "Meinke, give me five minutes on fishing," Swampy would thunder. I'd get up and say, "What sane person would go fishing?" or something like that, hoping for words to come up. "Who would stand around trying to torture a panicking wiggling worm, who never did anything to us, impaling it on a curved bit of steel?" "I would!" and "Boo!" the trapped audience shouted. We tended to make up long sentences to fill the time. But we learned to argue, make persuasive sense, and prepare carefully (especially in debate and longer speeches); and to not take anyone's statement at face value. Today, when our country's in trouble, bombarded by inflated advertising and misleading political "news," these are useful skills.

"Liber" in Latin means "free," and "liberalis" means "worthy of a free person." These words and values are the basis of Western democracy. This is an important battle: Wisconsin Governor Scott Walker sent in his budget, cutting the State University's funding by $300 million, proposing to change its motto from "the search for truth" to "meeting the state's work-force needs." Although he's since backed down (partially), it's clear, as a serious presidential contender, that he believes that's what the Republican voters want. I don't think he's right, yet, but if we cut the arts and humanities from our high school and college requirements, the truth will be much harder for Americans to find. (St. Pete's own Eckerd College is bucking this trend: They'll start building a new $12-million Center for the Visual Arts in May.)

John Adams is believed to have said, "I am a revolutionary so my child can be a farmer so his child can be a poet." Because of men like him, we're free citizens in a free country. It's up to us to keep American schools focused on the search for truth.

> *Can you   taste what I'm   saying?   .   .   .*
> *It stays in the back of your throat like a truth*
> *you never uttered because the time was always wrong,*
> *it stays there for the rest of your life, unspoken . . .*

> –both quotes from "The Simple Truth," by Philip Levine (1928-2015)

TANKER

MARCH 19, 2015

Oil on the Fire

*In Florida a mottled birdwatcher screeched brakes
to see an ivory-billed woodpecker banging away
on a dying bay Not many left Peter not many
left Forests shrink flocks disappear birdwatchers
worry where we're heading
but all over the hills the birdlike generals are
spreading*

He has the maniacal stare of Fatty Arbuckle, so it's impossible to look at Senate Majority Leader Mitch McConnell, flanked by his stern colleagues, without thinking of the Keystone Kops, reeling around in their open-topped police car and waving their batons with bug-eyed insanity. Around and around they go: the sheer repetitiveness is mind-boggling.

When the Republicans crushed the Democrats in November's midterm election, McConnell solemnly swore they could at last work together and get some important things done, avoiding the partisan divisions of recent years. So—with immigration, health, and budget bills begging to be addressed—what does he open with but a bill to approve the Keystone XL Pipeline, a clichéd example of a dirty energy source, and a guaranteed non-starter: the President had long ago pledged to veto it. So much for avoiding partisan divisions.

We already have more than enough oil. More oil is like more guns: we need some, but the more we have, the more accidents will happen. Trucks crash, ships hit rocks, wells explode, trains derail, and pipelines leak. Oil seeps from all of these, causing untold personal pain and permanent damage to our environment. Thousands of gallons of oil still pollute Alaskan waters from the 1989 Valdez ExxonMobil spill in Prince William Sound. The 2010 BP well blowout still poisons the Gulf of Mexico. Two major pipelines spilled last year (in North Dakota and Louisiana) and one already this year by the Yellowstone River. The Wall Street Journal reported 1400 pipeline spills from 2010-13. The damage and the litigation from all of these are multi-tentacled and unending.

President Obama has spoken—thoughtfully, not crazily—against the Keystone pipeline, which is not only small potatoes, but an unnecessary potato; and all the Republicans *really* want is for Obama to swallow it. But what we need now is a bill—a series of bills—to finally turn America toward facing climate change and the future. We should have started forty years ago. Kowtowing to the power of Big Oil, we let Japan beat us into the small car market, and it's beating us again with electric and hybrid cars. Europeans live in towns where its citizens can pop on trains to London, Paris, Berlin, or other countries. China, Germany, France and Japan offer their people high-speed long-distance rail systems. The Netherlands have built an incredible series of dams, dikes and windmills to protect their cities from the rising waters predicted for the future. Many nations—neighboring Nicaragua puts us to shame!—are making huge investments in unlocking the natural energies of the sun and wind.

Americans believe fiercely that we're the greatest country in the world. *We're Number One!* Well, let's buckle down and prove it. Let's bite the bullet and support the taxes needed to fund these programs, cutting our doomed dependency on oil, and invest our energy and ingenuity in making the next generations safer and healthier.

The Keystone Kops, famous for their frenetic incompetence, raced in all directions at once, bumping into each other at the corners. Still, this is America, where happy endings are *de rigueur* (to use an un-American phrase), and the Kops gradually morphed into supporting players for stars like Charlie Chaplin, Abbott and Costello, and others. It seems hopeless now, but I like to think that in 2016 someone will harness our Kongressional leaders, so instead of jackrabbitting all those jalopies they'll start turning windmills instead.

> *In Sunset Lake a thick pike trailing hooks and*
> *leaders bends stubbornly in diminishing circles*
> *jaw locked in a Nemonian smile Water tastes*
> *different now: so do fish Fishermen claim*
> *their schools are thinning*
> *but under all our seas the fishlike generals are*
> *grinning . . .*

–both quotes from "Generalsis I (1-3)" from *Lucky Bones* by Peter Meinke (U. of Pittsburgh Press 2014)

SCHOOL BUS IN FRONT OF OUR HOUSE

APRIL 2, 2015

Bus Story

There are badgers and bidgers and bodgers
and a Super-in-tendent's House
There are masses of goats, and a Polar,
and different kinds of mouse.

Around 10 a.m. one morning on April 5, 2007—during national poetry month—a huge yellow bus maneuvered the tight turns on Wildwood Lane and pulled onto the small park in front of our house. Big letters on its side said "Pinellas District Schools"—but what was it doing here? Maybe the driver stopped at the Chattaway and then got lost. Not likely, but we stepped outside to see if we could be of any help.

As we walked down our pathway the integrated faces of young students were smudged against the windows, like Monet's paintings of lily pads. A neatly dressed young man stepped out of the bus. His name was Bill Barlow, and he was taking his class of 4th grade students for a tour of the nearby Dali Museum. In his morning class on poetry, a student had asked, seriously, "Are all poets dead?" Good question.

He'd told them *No*, and said on the way to the Dali he'd show them the house of a real live poet.

"Should I let them pinch me?" I asked. "What school is it?" Maybe it was one of the schools our kids went to.

"Less than a mile away, on 22nd Avenue," he told me. "The James

Sanderlin School." That gave me goosebumps, and a flashback. It was poetic synchronicity.

The last time I'd been on a bus was in the summer of 1968 when I was gently dumped into one by two perspiring policemen, who were loading it with marchers supporting St. Pete's striking garbage men. Blocked by riot police as we approached City Hall, we sat down in the middle of the street. Driven to the Clearwater jail, we were fingerprinted, and crowded into cells with not enough beds and mattresses to handle the motley crowd of garbage men, students, teachers, and other supporters. Nevertheless, we spent the long hours singing "We Shall Overcome" and other songs, until bailed out by a young civil rights lawyer, Jim Sanderlin (1929-1990), who later became the first black judge in Pinellas County. He was a great and gentle person, who devoted his life to our city, and the cause of racial justice and equality. I felt honored to talk to the students at Sanderlin School.

I got on the bus and asked, "How many of you like to write poetry?" Basically, they all yelled "I do" with doubtful veracity but great enthusiasm.

"What big fibbers," I told them. "Fibbers," they cried. I told them when I was their age I wrote poems about bugs to scare my sisters. "Bugs!" they shouted. They were getting worked up. Some boy added "Boogers!" and I remembered repeating "Badgers and bidgers and bodgers" over and over, after reading A. A. Milne's "When We Were Very Young" for the first time, when *I* was very young. Milne's anarchical playfulness with language still delights me.

The children were now talking all at once, so we let them out of the bus to run around the park and use up some of that energy, creative or not. The school, Bill Barlow told us, was an IB (International Baccalaureate) Primary School. Its stated aim is "to recognize our common humanity," which I think is an unstated aim of poetry as well.

Some of the children were kicking up leaves in the gutter, uncovering a trove of wriggling night crawlers.

"It's a worm, ugh!"
"Don't pick it up, you'll get germs!"
Of course a little boy picked one up, but quickly flung it away.
"Worms, germs!" someone shouted, and others joined in.
A little girl said, almost thoughtfully, "Squirms."
Poetry lives.

And I think there's a sort of a something
which is called a wallaboo—
But I gave the buns to the elephant
when I went down to the zoo!

–both quotes from "Poem at the Zoo" by A. A. Milne (1882-1956)

SWEET BRIAR SIGN

APRIL 16, 2015

Sweet Briar

Bones in an African cave
gave the show away
they went violent to their grave
like us today

Our familiarity with Sweet Briar College came from three summers working at the Virginia Center for the Creative Arts, affiliated with the College and nestled nearby in bucolic Mount San Angelo. Novelist Sterling Watson and I used to enjoy a late afternoon run, down the hill from VCCA, across Route 29, around the historic buildings and tree-filled campus, past a groundhog who always popped out to greet us, and then back to our Center and its swimming pool: about a 7-mile round-trip.

One summer Jeanne came, too, with her own artist's studio where she pinned her lovely mini-drawings on the walls. That was the hot summer when the VCCA's water system broke down and we spent several waterless days in what was usually a pampered environment (watch out, California!). In the midst of this time, we received an invitation to an afternoon party from the president of Sweet Briar, Nenah Frey. The 20 male and female artists and writers formed, we imagined, the most ragged, sweaty, unshaved, odorous, hair-bedraggled group who ever marched across the immaculate Sweet Briar campus. As we crowded into the President's elegant living room like convicts released from hard labor, she received each one of us without blinking an eye. We sat around sipping sherry, while every ten minutes one of us would peel off and go to the bathroom, where we washed, shaved, combed our hair, and came back smelling a lot better. When we were all moderately presentable, we got up, thanked President Frey, hiked back up the hill, and went to work with a fond memory of Sweet Briar's immaculate *savoir faire*.

Now Sweet Briar, one of a dwindling group of all-girl colleges in the country, is closing its doors. It seems, despite its high quality, there's not enough interest in a rural school for girls. But all-girls colleges can offer a special education to their students in a free and safe environment: Barnard, Bryn Mawr, Hollins, Holyoke, Mills, Smith, Vassar, and others. I've twice been writer-in-residence at Converse College in Spartanburg, SC, and Jeanne and I admired its bright students, imaginative liberal arts program, and campus featuring statues of poet Emily Dickinson, artist Mary Cassatt, and singer Marian Anderson.

I attended all-boys Hamilton College in the 1950's, and it's clear that, after going co-ed in 1978, Hamilton's a more civilized institution today. But while co-ed undergraduate institutions are almost always better for boys, they're not always better for girls. When girls visited our campus in the old days, there were strict rules about where they could stay (which of course we constantly tried to subvert). The girls, however, were forewarned, or knew instinctively, that these were feral boys, and handled us easily while enjoying the adventure.

Today, with boys always around them—and a contemporary attitude toward sexuality—we have some alarming statistics (from the National Institute of Justice, U.S. Dep't of Justice, Campus Safety Magazine, and others): *20-25% of college women will be victims of attempted or actual rape*. These statistics have been questioned (by Fox News and others); but one statistic remains unquestioned: rape, whether in colleges, the military, or prisons, is vastly under-reported. I'm all for coed colleges, but I hope some all-girl schools hang in there, so we can study the different results. (See "The Hunting Ground," the new documentary about the FSU/Jameis Winston case.)

Our latest college scandal involves the Sigma Alpha Epsilon fraternity at the University of Oklahoma. The Greek motto of SAE is Συνδεσμοζ Αδελφων Εμμενοζκα, meaning "Everlasting Bond of Brothers." The Latin motto of Sweet Briar is *Rosam quae meruit ferat*, meaning "She who has earned the rose may wear it." There's a difference. I realize anything's possible, but it's hard to imagine a group of sorority sisters drunkenly, joyfully, chanting racist songs.

All things repeat
after the floods and flames
new boys play in the streets
their ancient games

    –both quotes from "Bones in an African Cave" by Peter Meinke (in *The Contracted World: New & More Selected Poems*, U. of Pittsburgh Press 2006)

RICHARD BLANCO

APRIL 30, 2015

Word Stars

When all the others were away at Mass
I was all hers, as we peeled potatoes.
They broke the silence, let fall one by one
like solder weeping from a soldering iron ...

–from "Clearances" by Seamus Heaney (1939-2013)

Once when we were in London the "Times" advertised a poetry reading by Seamus Heaney (pronounced Hee-ny) at a large theatre near Leicester Square. This was before 1995, when he won the Nobel Prize in Literature, but he was already well known, so after dinner we walked down Gower Street to hear him.

We were too late. In America, we're used to strolling into poetry readings at the last minute and finding room near the front, but the theatre was already packed. An excited babble of Irish and English voices washed over us as we stood in the lobby wondering if we could squeeze in. In the end, for the spillover crowd, they put his reading on the large television in the lobby, which had the advantage of also being where the bar was located. It was a wonderful reading.

Poetry's more popular all over Europe than it is in the States, but the Irish in particular love their poets. We've heard Irish cabbies, policemen, and bricklayers spontaneously recite poems by W. B. Yeats, James Joyce, and Cecil Day-Lewis (father of the actor Daniel Day-Lewis), often with a pint of Guinness in hand. My favorite uncle—my mother's high-spirited brother, Thomas McDonald—liked to jump on a table at parties to recite some sentimental (and occasionally scurrilous) verses.

Recently, Ireland voted on its "most-loved poem" of the last century. A committee of writers and teachers nominated ten poems out of 450 chosen by public ballot, and the public then voted again, for the winner. (A bit like our system in picking St. Pete's new pier, but different in that it actually worked.) The winner, a sonnet about his mother by Heaney—quoted above—was announced by the president of Ireland, Michael D. Higgins, to joyful applause.

Speaking of joyful applause, I'm happy to report that America's making strides in this direction. To celebrate National Poetry Month (April, because it includes Shakespeare's birthday), St. Petersburg College invited Richard Blanco to read here. Ever since Blanco read his poem "One Today" to the millions who watched President Obama's 2013 inaugural, he's been touring the country, bringing poetry to enthusiastic crowds. He read at St. Pete's Palladium to a large audience who paid $10 to get in—a rarity for American poetry readings—and gave him a standing ovation at the end.

Like Heaney's poem to his mother, Blanco's poems circle around family and fate, loaded with details that connect to larger vistas: "My mother's face should still be resting against / his bare chest like the moon resting on the sea." Of our inaugural poets, Blanco is the first immigrant, first Hispanic, first openly gay, and youngest. As he told the audience, he was conceived in Cuba, born in Spain, brought to New York before he was a year old, and then on to Miami's Cuban neighborhood when he was four. Now, that's a crackerjack springboard for a young poet.

Poets are always asking "Who am I?" and for Richard Blanco that's obviously an interesting and complicated question. Although he's lived his whole life in America, his poetry has the classic bittersweet taste of poets in exile, from Ovid to Derek Walcott. In addition, like two American poets he admires, Dr. William Carlos Williams and insurance executive Wallace Stevens, he's always held a "real" job, most recently as a civil engineer in Maine (about as far from lazy days in Key West that you can get). Throw in a sense of humor with the charisma of a star actor, and we have someone who, before he's done, may help create an enthusiastic audience for American poetry.

> *Where will I be buried? There's no place*
> *for me here. Who'll visit with flowers,*
> *speak to what's left of me? Yet I won't*
> *kiss his grave. Forgive me, Papá, bones*
> *that are my bones, teeth that are my teeth.*

> –from "Bones, Teeth" by Richard Blanco (in *Looking for the Gulf Motel*, University of Pittsburgh Press, 2012)

BOWL OF CHERRIES

APRIL 30, 2015

Our Lady of the Cherries

My supermarket is bigger than your supermarket   That's what America's all about   Nowhere am I happier nowhere am I more myself . . .

You can take America's pulse in our supermarkets. Upbeat, fearful, hopeful: These emotions float in the aisles, along with aromas from oranges, coffee, and Stilton cheese. A while back, around Christmas time, we were waiting on line to pay, and chatted with a young woman, admiring the cherries she had bought. After she checked out, the woman took the bag of cherries and, with a smile, popped it in our basket and walked away, shaking off our surprised protests. On the way home we kept talking about this generous present from a total stranger. We wondered if we had a saint in our neighborhood, and took to calling her "Our Lady of the Cherries." Although we've looked up and down the aisles, we've never seen her again. We have something to give her in return.

Downtown St. Pete is turning into a mecca of supermarkets (not to be confused with megamarkets like Walmart and Costco). Between the large Publix at 4th St. and 38th Ave. N. and the smaller one at University Village on the south side, we now have Rollin' Oats (2842 9th Ave. N.), The Fresh Market (2900 4th St. N.), Trader Joe's (2742 4th St. N.), and Locale Market (179 2nd Ave. N.). Plus others: Jeanne and I don't have time to stop at them all (a new one's scheduled to be built around 700 Central). And occasionally we run out to Mazzaro's Italian Market (2909 22nd Ave. N.) just to stand in front of its huge brick oven and murmur "*ciabatta,*" "*focaccia,*" "*pugliese*" . . .

These markets differ from one another, but the idea of a market being "super" is very American. They're big, clean, efficient, and they deliver the goods. Naturally, they're a major inspiration for our stories and poems. One of John Updike's greatest stories, "A & P," is set there. In Allen Ginsberg's poem, "A Supermarket in California," he meets Walt Whitman by the meat counters. The woman in Randall Jarrell's "Next Day" moves "from Cheer to Joy, from Joy to All." In place of Plato's "Allegory of the Cave," Stephanie Brown has written her popular American "Allegory of a Supermarket." My poem, above, began as a satire, but I wasn't halfway through before realizing how fond I was of our supermarket. It was a learning experience.

Like our gas stations, our supermarkets have a tendency to cluster together, like athletes elbowing for the best spot on the court. Everyone goes there: the seamstress, the mayor, the engineer, the unemployed, the alcoholic; a surprising number of shoppers arrive in wheel chairs. They provide a microcosm of America, in various outfits from formal jackets and ties to near nudity with tattoos, passing by the friendly checkout workers and smiling packers.

Sometimes this is unnerving, just standing on line and idly looking around. The magazines are *Woman's World, National Examiner, Stars, The Enquirer, People, In Touch, Life Style for Women.* Their headlines blare "Liz Taylor Died Broke," "Whitney's Daughter Suffocated," "Kate Rushed to Hospital," "Perfect Family Shocking Murder," "Leonard Nimoy's Secret Agony," "Oprah Fat Again." What makes one nervous is that these choices have been made after careful polling of the tastes of most buyers. Apparently no one impulse-buys "The Nation" or "The New Yorker." There's an un-American word to describe this: "*Schadenfreude,*" a German mouthful meaning the delight we feel when other lives aren't a bowl of cherries.

Life may be the pits for the rich and famous, but we're still looking for Our Lady of the Cherries, who cheered us up with her holiday gesture in our supermarket. We're hoping she may read this, and get in touch.

> *Listen friends Life is no rip-off the oranges are full of*
> *juice their coloring the best we can do why do you think*
> *we live so long?   So long*
> *My dear friends the supermarket is open Let us begin*

> –both quotes from "Supermarket," by Peter Meinke, in *Liquid Paper: New & Selected Poems* (U. of Pittsburgh Press 1991)

PAUL KRUGMAN

MAY 28, 2015

Healthy Choice

It is hard to have hope. It is harder as you grow old,
for hope must not depend on feeling good
and there's the dream of loneliness at absolute midnight . . .

It's been a long time since I've written anything about health care. Our own health, like most middle-class Americans', is holding steady —although I've been sneezing a lot lately—unaffected by the Affordable Care Act (ACA), aka "Obamacare," whose nickname's been appropriated by its supporters in the same way that "gay" has been by the LGBT community: OK, if you want to call it that, we'll take it.

But now that the 2016 presidential race is already bubbling like a sewer in Miami, and the Republicans have actually produced a sort of budget plan, I think it's time to assess the situation once again. The main reason is that the budgets I've seen are all based on repealing Obamacare (as well as dismantling other programs designed to help the needy).

One reason the GOP has presented so few new proposals over the years must be because they've spent so much creative energy— over 50 official efforts—to delay, gut, or repeal the ACA. Imagine how much better off the country would be if they'd used that time to help fix or adjust it. America has voted, twice, for Obama and his bill, but from the start Republicans have dug in against helping this black man whom they've refused to see, or even treat, as their leader. Ralph

Ellison's brilliant novel, *Invisible Man* (1952), should be required reading for Congress, not to mention our schools—but I doubt that Ellison's classic depiction of race in America is on many of the legislators' booklists (the ones who *have* book lists).

It's bizarre, for example, that Ted Cruz, the first to throw his sombrero into the presidential race, constantly brings up the old "birther" idiocy, saying things like "At least I know where I was born." (This takes chutzpah, as Cruz was born in Canada.) Another candidate, Ben Carson, calls Obamacare "the worst thing that happened to this nation since slavery." Lawyer it any way you want, they're playing the Nixonian race card, because in many places in America, including Texas, this card still plays well. Listen to the crowds when Cruz plays it. *Kenya!* (roar).

The cracked basis of Cruz's—and others—criticism is that Obamacare's bankrupting the country. Pete Sessions, chairman of the House Rules Committee, has claimed it costs $5 million per person. This kind of gonzo misrepresentation has been going on blatantly for years; and though it's been refuted by official reports like the Congressional Budget Office, and multiple essays by economists, including Nobel-prize winner Paul Krugman, it's swallowed whole by almost half the country.

When the ACA passed in 2010, Republicans predicted an immediate economic meltdown, including deficit explosion and job erosion *(job-killing Obamacare)*. Of course, since then—especially after Obamacare went into full effect—America has pulled out of the Great Recession better than most of Europe and Asia. Employment's gone steadily up, the deficit's been slowed, the stock market's booming, and the main trouble we have—lagging wages—stems not from Obamacare but from other complex and connected problems: elimination of blue collar jobs, weaker unions, outsourcing, a gutless tax system.

Even the setbacks with Obamacare, though real, have been superficial. One can blame the president for hiring incompetent technocrats to set it up, but that wasn't the fault of the ACA itself. And in the states where the Governors and legislators cooperated with the plan, it's going as well or better than could be expected of any huge operation.

But now our divided Supreme Court is about to decide—based on a four-word obvious oversight—the fate of a major part of the ACA: Can states, like Florida, that chose not to set up exchanges, decide not to accept federal subsidies, denying insurance to about 8 million people? Cross your fingers.

> *Find your hope, then, on the ground under your feet,*
> *your hope of Heaven, let it rest on the ground underfoot.*
>
> –both quotes from "A Poem of Hope" by Wendell Berry
> (in *Leavings*, Counterpoint Press 2010)

OUR DODGE

JUNE 8, 2015

Winter Revisited

One must have a mind of winter
To regard the frost and the boughs
Of the pine-trees crusted with snow . . .
Of the January sun; and not to think
Of any misery in the sound of the wind . . .

One sunny afternoon I decided to walk back to school. Because this was mid-January and we lived in St. Paul, Minnesota, the path was tunneled through an embankment of snow. There'd been a record-breaking snowfall, and I felt I was walking along a bobsled run. The sun bounced off the whiteness without warming.

No one was in sight, but suddenly I heard a familiar voice crying a faint "Help!" Squinting around in the glare, I saw our 5-year-old son Pete half buried in the snow. Of course I scrambled my way through and pulled out the remarkably calm but very cold youngster. Pete had been going to visit a friend but, already showing a preference for the path less traveled by, had decided to walk on the crusty top of the snow, which soon caved in; and he was stuck.

This is by now a family tale (*What if I hadn't decided to go back to school?* etc.). One reason we were walking is that our car was also stuck, buried in snow in front of our house. The car was safest that way.

Shortly before our grad school odyssey, a relative got us a deal we couldn't refuse on a newish used car: a ferociously finned pink and white 1957 Dodge Custom Royal Sedan with electric windows, which we sailed like Cleopatra's barge—that "burnished throne"—through the university towns of Ann Arbor and Saint Paul. It was so unlike us, it's a marvel we didn't break out in spots.

By the time Pete fell through the snow, we'd been through four Minnesota winters, and our massive vehicle hadn't survived well. We had no garage, and its underbody was rusting out: we could see the road through a hole in the passenger's side flooring. The back right electric window had died in the open position. The local Kroger Supermarket had helpful bagboys, and when one was carrying out some bags we told him to put them in the trunk as the back seat was full of snow. He laughed, thinking we were joking.

A larger problem was, before the city's snowplows buried it, on cold days our car seldom started anyway. On Saturdays I had an early morning class in Minneapolis. To start it, I usually had to walk a block to a friend's house, open his garage, pop the hood of his car, remove the glowing light bulb he kept on the battery to give it some heat, drive down the street to ours, attach the jumper cables, start the car, detach the cables, drive back, put the bulb back on the battery; and then run like hell back to our Dodge before it stalled again.

This was our wintry way of life. We seldom talked about it—it was just what we did—but when friends announced that they'd bought a Dodge Dart, I told them (as I've written before), well, we had a Dodge, but it wasn't exactly a Dart.

When we left for the flat but sunny landscape of Florida, we told everyone that we'd warm up for a few years and then return to civilization—but we never looked back. Fifty years later, we've become too thin-skinned, too soft, to even visit in the winter (last Christmas, we went to Hawaii). These memories of snowbound Pete and the frozen Dodge seem to belong to other people.

Of course, Florida has weather too; and as our soggy heat approaches, with its hurricanes and swelling tides, it can still remind us that nature has a mind of its own, and not for us.

Full of the same wind
That is blowing in the same bare place
For the listener, who listens to the snow,
And nothing himself, beholds
Nothing that is not there and the nothing that is.

    –both quotes from "The Snow Man," by Wallace Stevens, in *The Palm at the End of the Mind*, Vintage Books, 1972)

LAUREL LEAF

JUNE 25, 2015

Laureate

The poet laureate of the United States—PLOTUS, in the lingo—tends to be busy, Howard Nemerov once said, because he or she spends so much time explaining what the job entails.

–The New York Times, p. C3, 6/10/2015

I don't know if Senator Dorothy Hukill, a Republican from Port Orange, drinks or not, but all of us should pause during the cocktail hour and raise a glass in her honor. On April 23rd (Shakespeare's birthday), 2014, a bill she'd been fighting for became the law of the state. We know how difficult it seems to be for our legislators to pass anything, and this one had to do with a difficult subject as well: Poetry.

Florida, with SB 290 / HB 513, has joined 42 other American states by passing a law appointing a Poet Laureate for revolving three-year terms. Choosing me may not have been that sensible, but the law's a good one. Over time, a wide cross-section of Florida's talented poets will take turns representing our state, joining America's distinguished slate of state laureates: Robert Frost (VT), Gwendolyn Brooks (IL), Billy Collins (NY), Fred Chappell (NC), Vassar Miller (TX), Donald Hall (NH), Rita Dove (VA), Robert Bly (MN), and Natasha Trethewey (MI), to name just a few.

I was pleased, and also surprised. Florida's full of nationally known poets of all stripes, shapes and colors. As Jeanne and I have lived here since 1966, a high percentage of them are our friends, so we know that many are very well behaved.

The English poet Philip Larkin ("They fuck you up, your mum and dad. / They may not mean to, but they do") famously turned down a Laureateship because he dreaded "the sherry-drill with important people." But I'd worry more about sherry*less* drills, and our experience has been that there's always someone interesting there, important or not. Of course, Oscar Wilde's dictum comes to mind: "When the gods want to punish us, they answer our prayers." Although there were no campaigns (or even prayers) here, a lot of people wrote letters supporting me, and I want to tell all of you I'm honored and touched; and hope I can thank you individually.

As to what a state Poet Laureate actually does, I'll know a year or two down the line. While St. Pete's Poet Laureate I've read to school children, the City Council, the homeless; in libraries, colleges, parks with ex-Mayors Rick Baker and Bill Foster; at Studio 620, the Vinoy, Haslam's, Inkwood, Oxford Exchange, and the BookLover's Café.

The thing to remember is: *Poets come and go, but the poems are there when you need them.* Also, they can be fun. I enjoy reading them, reciting them, listening to them, memorizing them. Each night I fall asleep saying them to myself. This appointment will be much of a muchness, and I look forward to it.

Poetry lives by metaphor, telling us we're all connected. "Those are pearls that were his eyes," "For all the history of grief / an empty doorway and a maple leaf," "I should have been a pair of ragged claws / Scuttling across the floors of silent seas." Even if you don't believe in Her, nothing but God begins from scratch.

Our previous laureate, Ed Skellings, called himself the "electric poet." I'm perhaps one of the last "book" poets, loving books, journals, and the spoken word. Poetry's wonderful anywhere, but I love it best when printed on paper, held in my hand. I've never been as good as

I hoped, but in this hyped up, anti-reading environment, poetry's a *force* for good. Because it works indirectly, it doesn't reflect the party line and isn't selling anything. In metaphor we can find not only depth, but truth deeper than fact. As Emily Dickinson urges, "Tell all the Truth but tell it slant— / Success in Circuit lies":

> *As Lightning to the Children eased*
> *With explanation kind*
> *The Truth must dazzle gradually*
> *Or every man be blind—*
>
> –from poem #1129 in *The Complete Poems of Emily Dickinson* (Little, Brown & Co., 1960)

On June 5th, Peter Meinke was appointed Poet Laureate of Florida (PLOF, in the lingo).

JEB BUSH

JULY 9, 2015

Two Households

You whom I could not save
Listen to me.
Try to understand this simple speech as I would be ashamed of another.
I swear, there is in me no mastery of words.
I speak to you with silence like a cloud or a tree.

We're staring at the probability of another battle between two warring dynasties, Bush vs. Clinton, like the Capulets and Montagues in "Romeo and Juliet." Of course, the speeches were a lot better in Shakespeare's Verona: "From forth the fatal loins of these two foes / A pair of star-cross'd lovers take their life" sure beats "Well, I'm not a scientist." The worse thing is that while the lovers' tragedy lasts only two hours and may cost $200, this election cycle will take 16 numbing months, and cost well over the $6.3 billion price tag of the 2012 election (*Center for Responsive Politics*). With that kind of money, we could buy Verona, or even fix some of the problems our country faces.

To look at the leaders, both Hillary Clinton and Jeb Bush are money machines, but don't be fooled: these two dynasties are very different. The Bush money will go to fight climate change and restrict health care ("Obama care's a monstrosity"). It will suppress voters' rights (he purged 12000 eligible Florida voters while Governor), and reduce women's access to abortions (he pushed Florida's "Choose Life" license plates, not to mention his fierce interference in the Terri Schiavo case). Despite the Supreme Court ruling, he'd slow down the implementation of gay rights (fight "over the long haul," exhorts

| 195 |

Jeb), defuse unions, deflate the minimum wage, inflate the military, strengthen the NRA, and preserve tax breaks for the rich. These sound abstract but each one's sharp as Tybalt's sword, the literal tipping point of Shakespeare's play. And almost all the people who will bleed are poor.

Middle class and rich women will always get the abortions they need or want; poor women are being forced to bring unwanted children into a life of poverty (and often illness and crime), especially in states where Republicans have blocked everything from sex education to Planned Parenthood.

The thing is, Bush is the best Republican they've got. At this writing, Donald Trump's in 2nd place. Trump never changes and, like the Nurse in "Romeo," creates a comic effect (see SNL)—but, the fact that he's a popular contender tells you all about the Republican party you need to know. A vote for Bush is a vote supporting those dim multitudes who'd vote for Trump in the first place and cheer when he rails at the poor. Maybe he's just jealous. In the Bible, Matthew says "Blessed are the poor for theirs is the kingdom of heaven." No one ever says "Blessed are the rich for their children will inherit the earth tax-free."

Money may not be the root of all evil but it does have weight, like the sacks of marijuana that give Mexicans those muscular legs, à la Congressman Steve King. But instead of bulging calf muscles Republicans seem to develop rigid hearts. Year after year they elect men (almost always men) who, with their high salaries, slick insurance policies and lots and lots of vacation time, pass laws that utterly ruin the specific lives of the poor. They're strict on crime, too, and the connection between poverty and crime is obvious and ancient. Near the end of his play, Romeo's trying to buy illegal poison from a poor apothecary, who cries "My poverty, but not my will, consents."

It's hard to tell how Clinton will manage, but on all these policies affecting women and the poor, she'll be closer to helping than hurting them. With his party on his shoulders (like the immigrant's marijuana sack), even a moderate-leaning Bush won't be able to budge his party in the right direction. Besides, Bush's policies aren't as moderate as his demeanor. It's good he's polite, but that's not enough to help those in need.

> *What is poetry which does not save*
> *Nations or people?*
> *A connivance with official lies...*
>
> –both quotes from "Dedication" by Czesław Milosz (*Selected Poems*, The Seabury Press, NY, 1973)

EDGAR ALLAN POE

JULY 23, 2015

Wand'ring Minstrels

I do not like to apologize much
For these words, but I must. Such
Success as I have had has come
From carefully sitting loose and dumb,
Encouraging the gods to overlook me . . .

The gods in our country, as well as Americans in general, have often overlooked its poets. This usually doesn't bother our young bards, bent over their notebooks or computers, caught in the demanding grasp of their Muse telling them to write something, anything—*Now!* It says something about the state of poetry today that its ancient Muse, Calliope, called by Ovid and others the "Chief of all Muses," has had her name adopted by the least subtle of our musical devices, loud whistles driven by hot air for steamboats and circuses.

Most beginning writers tend to be bookish, maybe not exactly shy, but aware of their separateness from others. "From childhood's hour I have not been / As others were—I have not seen as others saw—" is the beginning of Edgar Allan Poe's poem, "Alone." Artists have odd interests and a skewed point of view, learning early to be generally quiet. They imagine themselves living their lives communing serenely or wrestling privately with this slippery Muse. Speaking in public just makes them nervous. (Hmm-mm: in certain ways, the closer we look at poets, the more they seem like everyone else.)

One odd development in a poet's life is, if she succeeds at all, she'll eventually find herself before groups of staring people while a microphone squeaks or burps as she leans her anxious head towards it. Singing for one's supper can be stressful. The French poet Arthur Rimbaud claimed poets discover their inner worlds by *dèréglement des sens* (disorienting one's senses), which in his days (1851-1894) they did by sipping absinthe. We have different potions to choose from today, but I think contemporary artists use stimulants less to help their writing than to get them through their public readings, and to relax *after* work.

Many artists frequent neighborhood taverns. Dylan Thomas headed to the White Horse Tavern in New York City (to which in our youth Jeanne and I made some memorable late night visits in his honor). Allen Ginsberg read "Howl" in Gallery 6 in San Francisco, the Dadaists gathered in Cabaret Voltaire in Zurich, James Joyce clicked glasses in Les Deux Magots in Paris, and Jack Kerouac unwound right here in St. Pete's Flamingo Bar. Needless to say, this *"dèréglement"* business can be carried too far, but there are few things more pleasant than relaxing with convivial friends after a hard day wrestling with the Muse (or presenting the results to a quizzical public).

One evening a poet named Hollis Summers (1916-1987) gave a lovely reading at a small college where I was teaching. We bought his book, shook his hand and went home. After a little while Jeanne asked, "Is anyone taking care of Hollis?" I was a young Instructor, and didn't know. Our chairman had delivered a fine introduction, but we guessed he—a quiet man himself—hadn't made any later plans, and left Hollis to fend for himself (it was late evening, after all). We knew they'd given him a spartan room in a nearby student dormitory (I'd picked him up for the reading), so I went over just to check. When I knocked on his door, it sprung open as if he'd been standing behind it. "Thank God you've come!" Hollis said.

Remembering who attended the reading, we called colleagues and students, who soon arrived with six-packs and high energies, and threw an impromptu party, using cheap beer instead of absinthe. The local Hamm's beer—"from the land of sky-blue waters"—was the popular choice. And the poets and poetry lovers, on many different levels, all agreed that Rimbaud, Poe, and Calliope would have approved.

> *So, a stanza's gone in excuses.*
> *Good. Counseling, like other abuses*
> *Of the mind, should always comprise*
> *Half truths plus half lies . . .*
> *But listen, lovers. Stay amateur.*
> *Try love, smiling, sober.*

> –both quotes from "Instructions for Two Serious Players" by Hollis Summers (in *VII Occasions*, Rutgers University Press, 1964)

JOHN KERRY

AUGUST 13, 2015

Nuclear Deal

Why do you live in prison
When the door is so wide open?

When the news came out of Vienna, the first thing we thought (somewhat childishly) was what a good time we once had there, sipping coffee at the Café Mozart near the great Opera House, not far from the neoclassical Palais Coburg where the negotiators had wrestled **passionately,** though comfortably, for such a long time. Perhaps influenced by this civilized setting, these seven diplomats have combined to shine a light on a brighter future, and we'd be foolish **to** turn away.

This is a world where peace is hard to find. Our own country is rife with suspicion and violence: Lafayette, Prairie View, Chattanooga, Charleston, Aurora, Newtown, Ferguson—our towns are getting known, not for their accomplishments, but for the blood spilled there. Anger and fear bubble on all sides, no place more fiercely than the Middle East, with Sunnis, Shiites, Arabs, Kurds, Turks, Armenians, and Israelis tangled in knotty hatreds reaching far back in time.

As with most windows of opportunities, this one—the Nuclear Accord with Iran—has been opened by a rare coming-together (like NASA's New Horizon flying by Pluto) that's not likely to happen again in our lifetimes. So intractable are our mutual problems and distrust, it seemed impossible that this steady slide toward antagonism and destruction could ever be slowed. And yet we have a chance to do that now.

The first miracle is that besides Iran and America, we have the signatures of Germany, Britain, France, Russia and China! When will it ever happen again? Second, we have two presidents, Barack Obama and Hassan Rouhani, that no one would have imagined ten years ago, both of whom have to battle powerful right-wing forces in their own countries. Obama, despite the Supreme Court upholding his programs, faces a congress dedicated to defeating anything he does. And Rouhani, a moderate reformist with a Ph.D. from Glasgow, has to deal with rigid theologians previously headed by his predecessor, the raving Mahmoud Ahmadinejad, and his unpredictable Supreme Leader Ayatollah Ali Khamenei. But Rouhani campaigned promising reforms at home and better relations with the West; and, with an educated pro-American population, this is now more possible than anyone thought. (It's probable that Jason Rezaian, the American reporter still held in an Iranian jail, was arrested as a spy by anti-American politicians in an effort to embarrass Rouhani).

Lining up with Obama and Rouhani were two indefatigable diplomats, both of whom in a better world would have been presidents of their countries, Secretary of State John Kerry and Iran's Foreign Minister Mohammed Javad Zarif. As they went back and forth to the hard-liners in both countries, months passing, deadlines falling, either one could have quit at any time; but back and forth they went, nursing a flickering flame.

Backing **them** were two brilliant scientists, Energy Secretary Ernest Moniz and Iran's Atomic Energy Chief, Ali Akbar Salehi, who—coincidentally and importantly—were together at M.I.T, Moniz as a faculty member and Salehi as a graduate student. They didn't know each other then, but their paths took the same swift trajectory. These two hammered out the technical aspects of the deal like a nuclear Rubik's cube.

The seventh man, who's been beside President Obama throughout the extended process, was Joe Biden, whose gift of good will and calming commonsense was invaluable; and is needed more as the Accord faces a skeptical and prejudiced Congress. (Just compare this team to its opponents, fearmongers like Netanyahu, Cheney, Krauthammer, Kristol, and their Republican friends, all of whom gave us the Iraq abomination.)

At the end, these talented negotiators—Obama, Housani, Kerry, Sarif, Moniz, Salehi, and Biden—handed us a seven-candled candelabra illuminating a possible way out of the wilderness. It wasn't easy for Moses (Exodus 26:31), and it won't be easy for us now. But we shouldn't be afraid.

> *Dance, when you're broken open.*
> *Dance, if you've torn the bandage off.*
> *Dance in the middle of the fighting.*
> *Dance in your blood.*
> *Dance, when you're perfectly free.*

–both quotes from "The Essential Rumi," translated by Coleman Barks (HarperCollins 1996)

CHRISTIE

AUGUST 20, 2015

Christie in Wonderland

There once was a turtle
Whose first name was Myrtle
Swam out to the Jersey shore.

The above words were the first lines of poetry I can remember, because back in the 1930's, when local accents were frowned upon, our grade school teachers in Brooklyn worked hard ("woiked hahd," we'd say) on erasing ours. Of course, we tended to bloit, "Dere once wuz a toitle ..." while the teacher would roll her eyes and ask us to repeat it, slower this time.

In 1945 we moved, against my teen-aged will, to what I called "Noo Joisey," then governed by Republican Walter Evans Edge, of whom I was totally oblivious, though much later he resurfaced (on TV) as a somewhat shady political pal of Nucky, the crime boss in "Boardwalk Empire." This leads, of course, to today's New Jersey Governor, the colorful and only occasionally shady Chris Christie.

In some ways, Christie's the anti-Obama, his very shape suggesting over-indulgence compared to President Obama's disciplined leanness. When they walked together through the wreckage of Hurricane Sandy, they brought to my mind the 1939 Trylon and Perisphere in New York's World Fair, the tremendous girth of the Perisphere the perfect foil for the towering skinny Trylon—connected by the world's longest escalator—a wonder for my then seven-year-old eyes.

And this summer, when Christie threw his oversize hat into the Republican presidential ring, he once again nudged me back into my early years. "I'm running for President," he said (repeatedly), "and one thing you will know for sure: I say what I mean, and I mean what I say."

Hasn't Christie ever read "Alice in Wonderland"? Those are the same words Alice says at her famous tea party with the March Hare and the Mad Hatter, adding "That's the same thing, you know."

"Not the same thing a bit!" says the Hatter. "Why, you might just as well say 'I see what I eat' is the same thing as "I eat what I see." Needless to say, an uncomfortable conversation for Christie, who seems not to have properly digested it.

I hope Christie's numbers go up in the polls, because he's fun to watch. The media exploits his directness, delighting in replaying his explosions: "None of your business!" he'll shout, or "Sit down and shut up!" Many of the times, to viewers who've seen longer segments, these seem justified, or at least normal: Who hasn't wanted to tell off an obnoxious antagonist?

That's why I was disappointed in his reaction to the Trump phenomenon. The Donald lives in a fantasy world stranger than Tweedledee and Tweedledum's, and Christie's smarter than Trump in almost every way; but he missed a great opportunity by declaring him a friend, instead of a bloated bigot. In addition, in Christie's debate argument with Rand Paul, he started off with, and repeated, a Trumpian and colorless falsehood: "I was appointed U.S. Attorney the day before the September 11th attacks." Check Politifact: He can lie better than that.

Most mornings we watch at least some of "Morning Joe," rooting for Mika Brzezinski to act a bit like Christie and tell Joe to clam up and listen. It was fun seeing Christie on the program attack the media for making him out to be "Attila the Hun" during the Bridgegate scandal. But this presidency business is making him curb his tongue.

His polling numbers, even in New Jersey—maybe especially in New Jersey—are lower than Governor Scott's in Florida. And if he's not being up front and outrageous, what's he have to offer? Although unlike Scott, he's accepted Medicaid for New Jersey, and has tempered his stance against gay rights, Christie's now trying to edge far enough to the right so he can get invited to the Party, and like Lewis Carroll's original scene, his offerings are all weak Tea.

> *"Have some wine," the March Hare said in an encouraging tone. Alice looked all round the table, but there was nothing on it but tea. "I don't see any wine," she remarked. "There isn't any," said the March Hare.*
>
> –from "Alice's Adventures in Wonderland" by Lewis Carroll (1832-1898)

THE HURRICANE

SEPTEMBER 3, 2015

Root Causes

Hell hath no limits, nor is circumscrib'd
In one self place, where we are is Hell,
And where Hell is, there must we ever be.

The other evening we watched a spectacular sunset from the top of the Hurricane on St. Pete Beach, and I thought of Doctor Faustus towards the end of Christopher Marlowe's old (1604) play. I looked around at our fellow customers and tourists, enjoying the view, with margaritas and grouper sandwiches, far from the atrocities of ISIS, Kenya, Nigeria, Syria, even the man who threw his daughter off the Skyway Bridge that we can see from up here. Like most of them, despite reading about these things every single day, we feel reasonably happy—but still can't help thinking (knowledge is guilt) of doomed Faustus who, having sold his soul, looks up and sees a scarlet sunset similar to the one we're gazing at now, and cries *See, see, where Christ's blood streams . . .*

Living in the Internet age means we're always dealing with the current calamity, real, exaggerated, or truly catastrophic: earthquakes, assassinations, kidnappings; planes dropping like flies, children sold by the hour. Large areas of the world are toxic, and we as a country seem to get dragged into them, for good and bad purposes. But we as *people* live in a bubble more impenetrable than the gated communities of the wealthy.

These disasters have always happened—many, perhaps most,

without our knowing it. But now we're all like numbed security guards in a room full of cameras monitoring the latest abominations: beheadings, stonings, drownings, burnings, murders live on TV. Knowledge is power, they used to tell us. Now it seems more like knowledge is tragedy. But that's an exaggeration: maybe knowledge today is just anxiety. The Age of Anxiety, predicted by W. H. Auden's poem in 1947, has truly arrived.

One reason we feel anxious is that so many things happen so quickly in so many places that we don't know where to start. Probably we need to take a deep breath, go back in our heads, and look for root causes. That's where some real work can actually be done, which is why the Iranian Nuclear Treaty would be a step in the right direction. ISIL, al-Qaeda, al-Shabab, Boko Haram, Hezbollah, the Taliban, can hurt individual Americans, but not America. Decent human beings live in all the countries from which these groups spring, and somehow we need to reach out: Bombing, fighting, starving them only spreads the poison. ISIS is the offspring of Guantanamo, the grandchild of Abu Ghraib, the great-grandson of My Lai.

Closer to home, one of our country's crises has been the overrunning of our southern borders—often by children, mimicking the perhaps apocryphal and also disastrous original Children's Crusade (1212), when European Christians and their children marched out to expel Muslims from the Holy Land. Our politicians have gone bonkers, some blaming President Obama, others saying they're coming here to sell drugs or live free off our government. Governor Perry sent in the Texas National Guard to protect us from these youngsters. No one, least of all Donald Trump, seems to be asking why they're crossing the border and surrendering to the first persons they meet, throwing their young lives into our hands.

Peeling the layers backward, through the poverty and violence, we arrive at the root causes of this exodus: our hunger for drugs, which has rendered these children's cities unlivable; and our business leaders' drive for cheap labor, which has brought the adults over to sweat for pennies in the shadows.

At about the same time as Auden's poem, Walt Kelly's Pogo said, "We have met the enemy and he is us." We used to turn to the church, and many still do (these days, Pope Francis is an inspiring figure). For others, turning to art, including the comic pages, might temporarily soothe and stimulate their minds.

> *See, see where Christ's blood streams in the firmament.*
> *One drop would save my soul, half a drop, ah my Christ.*
>
> –both quotes from *Doctor Faustus* by Christopher Marlowe (1604)

BOONTON WARE

SEPTEMBER 17, 2015

Odd Jobs

*All night at the ice plant he had fed
the chute its silvery blocks, and then I
stacked cases of orange soda for the children
of Kentucky, one gray boxcar at a time . . .*

Danny Lawless, editor of the online poetry journal *Plume*, had the idea of asking poets to briefly describe the oddest or most memorable job they ever had; and he got a lot of fascinating replies. It's delightful to think of Jane Hirschfield driving a truck.

As a closet pacifist, I suppose being a soldier was my strangest. The Korean War had just ended—I was drafted right after graduation, in 1955—and most Americans thought the draft was fair. America wasn't much involved in Vietnam yet, so the closest I came to shooting anyone was in 1956 when Russian tanks rolled into Budapest, crushing the Hungarian freedom fighters. I was with an infantry division in Würzburg, Germany, about 400 miles away; and our sergeant was jumping-up-and-down happy as we cleaned our M1s. (Years later I read poetry at the University of Budapest, and the freedom-loving students crowded around, most of them asking, "Do you know Allen Ginsberg?" They couldn't believe anyone could write a book like *Howl* without getting arrested. "I've shaken his hand," I told them, trying to look modest.

The 1950's were patriotic days: despite an occasional doubt (Hiroshima?), we felt in general that America did the right things. The

Vietnam War changed all that. But that's another subject. So, leaving out the grand topics of war and peace, I held my most memorably odd job during a long summer four years before I was drafted.

At that time, earning money for college, I worked at the Boonton Molding Company, in Boonton NJ, making plastic dishes. The molding room was a scene out of Dante's Inferno. Gleaming breathing machines hissed up and down, workers hunched in front of them transferring compressed-powder disks like hockey pucks from a small oven to the molding machine, and then punched the button to bring the forms together to mold the plate, saucer, or cup. When the mold opened you had to pluck out the red-hot piece with a suction cup, drop it in a tray, pick up the disk, put it in its oven, smooth the rough edges of the plate or cup; and start the whole process again. We were paid by piece-work, and the men worked very fast.

The heat was fierce, no doubt illegal today, and all of us were soaked within minutes. This was before air-conditioning and the windows had to be closed because floating dust might get into the machine and stain the finished product: pale-colored plates, saucers, and cups, thick but unbreakable and charmingly shaped—they're collectors' items today.

There were eight machines, and once an hour I'd slow down mine and run out and get eight cokes. (The men were so fast they could reach over and keep my machine going, at a slower pace.) I was the only boy—an executive at the company, a golfer I caddied for, got me the job; and the men treated me well, like a pet. They kidded me because I worked the swing shift (8-4, 4-12, 12-8) and I'd arrive in everything from pajamas to evening clothes. Their guesses as to how I spent my days and nights were delightfully obscene and, alas, far off base.

After my stint, I'd change near the loading dock (there was no shower). Occasionally a police car would slide by. A policeman who had watched our high school games would get out and wave, and I'd toss him a cup or scale a plate, and then duck back inside, feeling very grown up. At the time, the men seemed old to me, but at least one of them, as well as the man I caddied for, died in Vietnam.

> *... We were twenty*
> *for such a short time and always in*
> *the wrong clothes, crusted with dirt*
> *and sweat. I think now we were never twenty.*
>
> –both quotes from *"You Can Have It,"* by Philip Levine (1928-2015), in *New Selected Poems*, Random House 1991

DESTROYING ANTIQUITIES

OCTOBER 1, 2015

Whiz, Bang!
The Nuclear Accord

There was this terrific battle.
The noise was as much
As the limits of possible noise could take.
There were screams higher groans deeper
Than any ear could hold.

The opponents of the Iran Nuclear Accord rightly claim that their "strong opposition conveys an important message to the world," but they're dead wrong about the actual message. The immediate 100% rejection of this 159-page document by the entire Republican legislature only showed, yet again, that they'll oppose anything President Obama proposes. Why pretend this is reasoned debate, or any debate whatsoever? It's like Tom Brady, a fan of Donald Trump, pretending he didn't know there was less air in the football. The Republican vote was 300 to 0.

Engulfed by a tsunami of misleading ads, the Democrats nevertheless squeezed out enough votes to carry the day. Senators complained about "minority rule," but Obama was twice elected by an ungerrymandered majority, and this is what he was elected to do. The world—we're joining the other major nations (and Pope Francis) on this—is proud of America again, recognizing what we tend to forget: Obama is the leader of the free world.

It took courage for Florida's first Jewish representative, Debbie

Wasserman Schultz, to vote for the measure, as did Senator Bill Nelson and Representatives Kathy Castor, Alan Grayson, Patrick Murphy, Frederica Wilson and Corrine Brown. We should thank them all.

Almost half our country's energy seems focused on breaking things down instead of building new foundations. David Brooks picks up on this while explaining the Trump phenomenon: Trump, he wrote, isn't so much a leader as "an expression of his followers' id." Considering Trump in Freudian terms (id, ego, superego) is a fine idea, but Brooks doesn't go far enough. (Quick reminder, roughly: id = our irrational, often destructive urges; superego = our moral constructive conscience; ego = the mature rational mediator between the two.)

Think of ISIS, smashing the icons of antiquity, as the id of Islam, out of control and given full reign. The far right wing is the id of the GOP, not yet in control but dangerous to the party and the country. In a democracy built on a unifying affirmative vision, this minority wants, besides wrecking the Iran deal, to repeal Obamacare, expel the immigrants, crush the unions, deny climate change, refuse gay marriage, eliminate gun control, defund Planned Parenthood, undo voting rights, close the Cuban embassy, cut programs supporting the poor, hinder equal pay, restrict women's rights, and shut down the government. They even complained when Obama had dinner with China's Xi Jinping, and erupted when he restored the original Indian name, Denali, to Mount McKinley (named for a Republican president who never visited the mountain). On the eve of Pope Francis's visit, George Will, a major Republican pundit and passionate champion of the Iraq war, attacked the Pope's "fact-free flamboyance."

Michelle Goldberg (author of *Kingdom Coming: the Rise of Christian Nationalism*) recently said America's "in a period of racial animus." I don't see any *kristallnacht* or mass lynchings in our near future, but when a loudmouth orator gets a crowd worked up by insulting immigrants and women, it's a dangerous sign. And there's Mike Huckabee, weeping in front of a crowd supporting Kim Davis as she emerged from jail. Davis came out and cried, "Never give up this fight!"

America's main problem may be that it doesn't yet realize we *are* in a fight.

Whiz bang! How much faster and easier to destroy instead of build! How good Jimmy Carter looks, in his last few years, as he builds houses with Habitat for Humanity all over the world. Despite his occasional spurt of lust, Jimmy Carter's looking more noble as he ages. Noble is as noble does.

> *And when the smoke cleared it became clear*
> *This had happened too often before*
> *And was going to happen too often in future*
> *And happened too easily . . .*

—both quotes from "Crow's Account of the Battle," in *Crow*, by Ted Hughes (1930-1998), published by Harper & Row, NY 1971

NYC CAB

OCTOBER 15, 2015

Taxi!

Recently we decided, too late to get decent airfare, to duck the end of the rainy season and make our yearly breakaway to NYC. When we got to the City, we made another decision. Our hotel was on the Upper West Side, near Central Park and the Museum of Natural History; the subway map showed us we could get there without changing trains. Climbing out of a ragged Penn Station, we saw the MTA (Metropolitan Transportation Authority) signs plastered all around but, feeling a bit guilty, took a cab instead.

We realized right away that we had crossed a certain divide, and were going to see New York as an elderly well-off couple. ("Rich" would be the wrong word, but we now can afford to take taxis in New York. We've paid off our mortgage.)

Jeanne grew up in New Jersey, but early on worked at Adelaar Fashions in the City. I lived in Brooklyn, and regularly rode the trains and trolleys. When living elsewhere we enjoyed the London tube, the French Metro, the Neuchâtel trams, the Bangkok skytrain, the Provincetown ferry, and the Polish buses (huge folding affairs, made in the Netherlands). *No problemo*, as schoolkids say.

But last year, when we headed down the wormhole of the Big Apple's subway, our stomachs clenched a bit. Newspapers and candywrappers blew around, the walls were chipped and peeling, the handrails (we hold onto handrails now) coated with gum and other unidentified but alarming substances. Buying the tickets was a complex job (for us), and even getting them to work in the turnstiles was tricky—and not just for us: a mature woman nearby gave up swiping her card, gathered her long dress about her, and stoically clambered over the bar. No one seemed to notice. There were other problems (Is this the express train? etc.), but those were our main impressions. In addition, a few friends have witnessed violent subway episodes, though we've never seen one.

So, taking a taxi was a relaxing and reliable experience; usually, though not always, much faster. The taxis were clean, the meters clear, the drivers—every one a minority male—amazingly skillful, constantly making those necessary merges with inches to spare. Our last one, named (we think) Zané, was a sit-down comic from Trinidad. We felt like applauding when we disembarked.

Unbeknown to us in the beginning, we were witnessing a change in New York taxis, though it didn't register right away. We rode—they were far more numerous—in the usual New York "muscle cab," the big tough-looking Ford Crown Victorias, for decades the prototype NYC cab (á la Jeanne's drawing) with its tough but lively drivers. But we noticed a small number of more foreign-looking taxis, same color, shorter and boxier, with a much bigger yellow "T" in a black circle stamped on its door. We weren't keen on this look, which we learned was the Nissan NV200, scheduled to replace the Crown Victorias starting this fall (Mayor Bill de Blasio campaigned against it, but lost).

Well, I guess this will be progress. The Nissan, advertised as the "Taxi of Tomorrow," apparently has more leg room, along with a sunroof, sliding doors, and cell-phone-charging outlets. Again, this must be our age: Jeanne and I don't carry gadgets to charge, don't go to New York for sunshine, and our legs are shrinking. Plus, in our experience, sliding doors can be a menace to fingers.

Anyway, good experiences, like art or love, aren't always comfortable.

Of course, there are some other things we'll miss in our upscale transportation plans. I'll close with a familiar sight at the Times Square Subway Station. In 1991 the MTA paid an artistst/photographer $5000 for the installation, "A Commuter's Lament, or a Close Shave," each line on its separate beam, in a parody of the old Burma Shave highway ads. It was supposed to be temporary, but just look up: Like many other poems, it's still hanging in there.

Overslept
So tired
If late
Get fired
Why bother?
Why the pain?
Just go home
Do it again

    –by Norman B.Colp (1944-2007)

BERNIE SANDERS

OCTOBER 29, 2015

Bernie Sanders

How many dawns, chill from his rippling rest
The seagull's wings shall dip and pivot him,
Shedding white rings of tumult, building high
Over the chained bay waters Liberty—

Confirmed escapists, Jeanne and I have always been movie-lovers, so it's normal for me, while waiting for small change from a twenty, to think like a curmudgeon: I remember when movies cost 11 cents for a double feature, with serials, cartoons, and news (*The Eyes and Ears of the World!*)—without 20 minutes of deafening and mentally degrading previews.

This was at the Nostrand Avenue Theatre in Flatbush, so I got a pleasant jolt when I read that young Bernie Sanders spent his Saturdays in the same place at about the same time. He lived on 26th Street, not far from 32nd, where I grew up. We never met because the Meinkes moved to Noo Joisey in 1945—unless that was Bernie handing out leaflets while pedaling his tricycle along the Brooklyn sidewalks (I'm nine years older). So I'm glad to read about Sanders, and if he were nominated we'd vote for him in a blink.

Still, I'm not on Team Bernie, even though it's just Hillary and him now. He's been drawing great crowds, but while encouraging, this isn't enough to lead the Democrats in 2016, because Sanders is basically a European-style socialist. Bernie may be ready but America isn't. Maybe 20% are, and that's progress. Still, considering how close the country's split on the Affordable Care Act, you can get the idea of the gulf that needs to be cleared.

There's a big money gap, too, but hopefully neither the noise on the Republican side (Donald Trump) nor the noise on the Democrat side (Sanders) will make a difference in the end, when they'll both disappear. But the lesson to take away from this divide is the difference between the two noise-makers:

This is exactly the difference between the heart of these two parties.

Though both would object, in actual effect one is socialist and one is racist. Democrats keep edging toward a system, well, more like Denmark's. Higher taxes for the rich and more programs for the poor. And though Republicans can hold up their hands and say, "That's not me," all around the country, every day, the GOP is working to limit the black vote, and to make life harder for immigrants, especially immigrants of color.

Regarding policies, there's little wiggle room between Clinton and Sanders: they'd pretty much vote the same way, as Sanders keeps pulling Clinton leftward. This is good for all of us, though the TPP is more complex than most people, remembering NAFTA, believe. But in complicated arrangements, I'm willing to give the nod to Obama, who says that TPP is at least partly designed to reverse the negatives of NAFTA. Set attitudes can change radically with new developments: Remember how we loved The Cosby Show (set, oddly enough, in Brooklyn)?

Also, Clinton has been better at resisting the NRA and defending Planned Parenthood than Sanders, who—like everyone else, including Clinton—was upset by the nasty and visceral video the Republicans are circulating. But Clinton truthfully pointed out that, unpleasant as that video is, over the years Planned Parenthood has changed the lives of thousands of women for the better, and actually saved many of them.

The subtitle of St. Pete writer Peter Golenbock's lively book about Brooklyn—*In the Country of Brooklyn*—is "Inspiration to the World." Bernie Sanders, a rare honest and idealistic politician, fits that description.

So he has my best wishes, and if we ever meet we could talk about Prospect Park, stickball, the Dodgers, and all those good delicatessens in Flatbush. He'd be a fine president; but when he doesn't get nominated, he won't pull a Nader and run independently. Most likely he'll keep pushing Clinton to the left, while poking holes in Republican balloons.

> *O sleepless as the river under thee,*
> *Vaulting the sea, the prairies' dreaming sod,*
> *Unto us lowliest sometime sweep, descend*
> *And of the curveship lend a myth to God.*

–both quotes from "Proem: To Brooklyn Bridge," by Hart Crane (1899-1932), Liveright Publishing Co, 1958

POPE FRANCIS PRAYING

NOVEMBER 12, 2015

A Tale of Two Popes

O goodum! Habemus Papam
who'll soon intone
the usual crapum

and the poor poor will weepum

and the rich will yawn
and eatem
like pablum

    This may astound you, but poets and their poems are sometimes just plain wrong, as when John Keats, in his sonnet, "On First Looking Into Chapman's Homer," has "stout Cortez," instead of Balboa, staring out at the Pacific; or Longfellow, in "The Landlord's Tale," has Paul Revere, "a shape in the moonlight," riding alone (there were three riders), etc.
    My mistake in "Habemus Papam" (Latin for "We Have the Pope") was one of prediction. I didn't guess that Pope Francis wouldn't preach the "usual crapum" but would instead be a fresh voice signaling a more inclusive Catholic Church. Father, I confess I was wrong about that. The new Pope's demeanor was underlined because while he was gently saying—even to John Boehner—"Pray for me," Donald Trump was shouting to everyone, "Look at me!"
    Jeanne and I have some experience in this Pope business. In

1978-79 the Meinke family lived in Warsaw, when two major events pulled the Poles, smothered by their hated Russian bosses, out of despair and depression: first, Isaac Bashevis Singer won the Nobel Prize for Literature, and then an ex-professor and poet, Cardinal Karol Wojtyla, became Pope John II, the first non-Italian Pope since the 16th Century. Poland's a Catholic country, its religion inseparable from its politics, so they went bonkers. (Once I asked a Polish colleague why the church crosses were always lit at night. "It's not for Jesus," he said. "It means that Poland is still fighting.")

Just as Pope Francis may be a catalyst for social/sexual changes in church doctrine, John Paul II was a catalyst in the collapse of Communism, and galvanized Poland to shake off the Russian bear hug. Jeanne and I saw him lift the Iron Curtain with his bare upraised hands.

In the spring of 1979 rumors began to fly through the streets of Warsaw: the new Pope—a Polish Pope!—was going to visit Poland. Nothing was in the papers (nothing important or true was ever in the papers). It was all word of mouth, wildly speculative. Would the Russian dictators let him come? Would they let the people see him? Then one day, suddenly, all the liquor stores in Warsaw were closed, and everyone knew: Pope John Paul II was on the way!

On June 2nd the Pope arrived. Poland was "roped off" into sections, in order to keep the whole country from traveling to Warsaw. By 8:30 a.m. the streets were lined 10 deep around Victory Square, many wearing colorful and heavy peasant costumes in the summer heat.

With smuggled tickets from a friend, we slowly wiggled our way to the Square by the afternoon, and witnessed the whole event. An estimated 3 million people spread out from the Square—the largest outdoor Mass in the history of the Church: loudspeakers everywhere, soldiers nervously lined up in the alleys in case the people began to march. They didn't then, but at the same time, listening on the radio in Gdansk, Lech Wałesa and the dock workers were printing posters and unrolling their Solidarity banners. Pope John Paul raised his hand: The people began chanting, in that huge Square named for the Soviet victory in World War II, "We want God! We want God! . . ." SOLIDARNOSC was born.

* * * *

In my poem's defense, I'll point out that, though Francis has been mostly pushing for the "right" things, so far not much has actually changed. The Church remains fabulously wealthy and corrupt, and with its rules on abortion and the place of women, the "poor poor will weepum" for the foreseeable future. But somewhere some nuns may be circled together, like Wałesa and the workers, and who knows what they may be knitting?

"Habemus Papam" by Peter Meinke, first appeared in "The Tampa Review," and is in his book *The Contracted World*, (U. of Pittsburgh Press, 2014)

ELF ON A SHELF

NOVEMBER 26, 2015

Elf-Employment

Poems are, a little bit, like elves
Who peek-a-boo among your shelves
And make up rules to please themselves.

When I was a little boy, my German grandfather—usually after a manhattan or two—would often lead me up the steps of his Brooklyn home to a large wall poster with colorful drawings, to give me a little German lesson. *Ist das nicht eine schnitzelbank?* he'd ask, pointing at a cobbler's bench, or if it were Christmas, he'd point at a Christmas tree, saying *Ist das nicht ein Tannenbaum?* I'd answer faithfully, *Ja das ist ein Tannenbaum*, or whatever picture he'd point at. Sometimes we'd try to sing the chorus, *O, Die Schoenheit an der Wand* (O the beauty on the wall)—*Ja das ist eine schnitzelbank*.

It was fun, contributing to my early love of picture books and children's poems (and maybe manhattans). I particularly liked it when he'd point at the drawing of a *schnickel fritz*—a naughty boy—and say, giving me a poke in the ribs, "*You* are a *schnickel fritz*, Peter," and I'd squeal in mock protest, *Nein, ich bin ein gutter junge!*" He usually gave me a quarter, whether I was good or not. I certainly wasn't a *gutter* singer.

As far as I can remember, I've always liked poems and picture books, and scribbled (nonsense of course) as soon as I learned to read and could hold a pencil. The Schnitzelbank song is my earliest memory of liking rhyme, rhythm and pictures together. I'm still a constant doodler, as my notebooks show.

Of course, my mother must have sung lullabies to us; she was a pianist with perfect pitch. But my memories of her are almost all at the piano. The first actual poems that still have their prints in my head are from three little books, *When We Very Young* and *Now We Are Six* by A. A. Milne, and *A Child's Garden of Verses* by Robert Louis Stevenson.

Milne, of course, is best known for his Winnie-the-Pooh books—early versions of Pooh appear in his poems. The books we had were small, one red and one green, and, like the Pooh books, were brilliantly illustrated by E. H. Shepard. A theory of mine is that as a child, T. S. Eliot also loved Milne and Shepard, which is why he called himself, copying their practice, "T.S" instead of "Tom" or Thomas Eliot. (My early poems were signed "J. Peter Meinke," but after a few years I dropped the "J" (for James) as looking too much like "J. Alfred Prufrock.")

Shepard's charming drawings are immediately attractive and accessible, and they look easy to do—but having watched Jeanne working on her own pen and ink drawings, I know that this isn't the case. Like anything well done, hard work, practice, and training—and a great deal of time—go into each drawing. When Jeanne was working on the elves in our latest book, it was amazing to see the metamorphosis of the little rascals as she worked on creating them. A lot of crumpled paper on the floor, and suddenly, there's Pooh on a page, with his hand in the honey, or Jeanne's elf doing a handstand on a bookshelf.

Where does creativity come from? The seeds go far back, to gruff grandfathers, beloved pets, early dreams, generous teachers—but the plants themselves need to be watered, trimmed, and constantly tended.

Now, elfin poets, girls and boys,
  These rules draw to a close;
Please go to bed and no more noise
  Or else I'll tweak your nose!

  –both quotes are from *The Elf Poem* by Peter Meinke,
   illustrated by Jeanne Meinke, published by the U. of Tampa
   Press, 2015

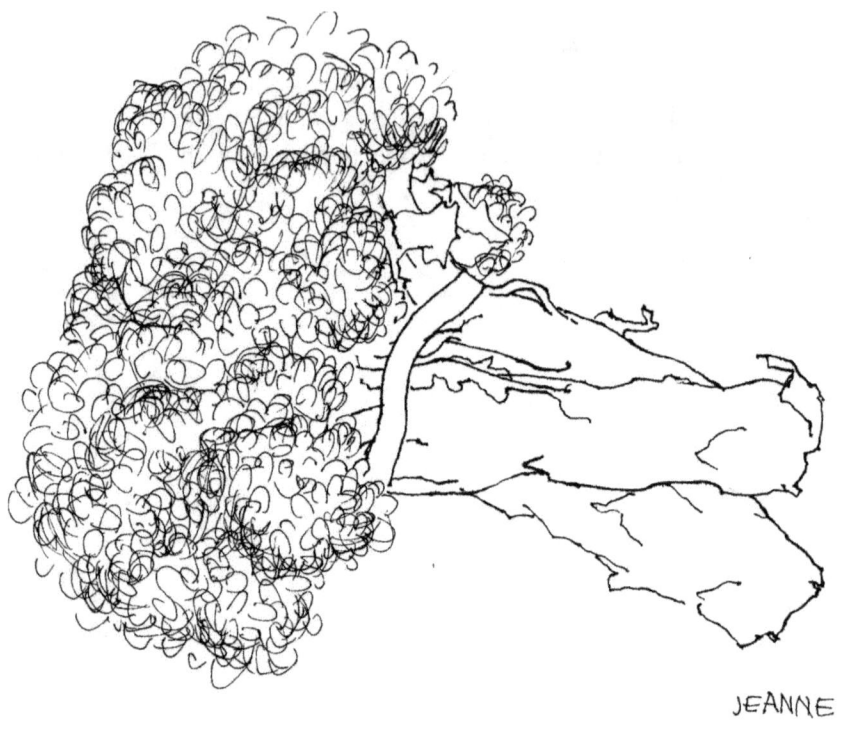

BROCCOLI

DECEMBER 17, 2015

Poetry & Broccoli

It was many and many a year ago,
  In a kingdom by the sea,
That a maiden there lived whom you may know
  By the name of Annabel Lee . . .

Several friends have noted that, generally speaking, they enjoy hearing poetry when it's read to them, but not so fond of it on the page. Buying a book of poems would be a rare occasion. Of course, *anyone* buying a book of verse is pretty rare in America, as its musty corner in any book store pronounces: *Abandon all Hope, Ye Who Enter Here.* Why a poetry book cover might resemble the gates of hell has a long history, but let's try to stick to the reading/hearing problem.

In a way, poems in a book are like musical notes on a page. They play in your mind, but as with musical notes, there are infinite ways they can be played, depending on the reader's talent, experience, and mood at the time. The problem students have, I learned, is that they tend to read poems too quickly (which after all is the American way—life in the fast tweets). One has to learn to read poems slowly, trying to feel out the form, the tone, the sounds, the sense. When you hear a poet read her own poems, all these things wash over you at once, like music. If it brings you near tears, it isn't so much the "story," but the overall experience, like a Mozart Requiem or a Bach Chorale. A large part of this kind of enjoyment is a recognition, often subconscious, of something well done; one can react that way to a painting, or a dance, or some amazing athletic feat.

Edgar Allan Poe had the right idea when he scandalized the New England poets by claiming that poetry wasn't a moral lesson that was "good for you" ("like broccoli," as I was recently quoted as saying on NPR), but an aesthetic experience; Poe defined poetry as the "Rhythmical Creation of Beauty." He didn't say poetry couldn't teach morals, but this wasn't its main job.

Ralph Waldo Emerson responded by calling Poe "the jingle man." There's something right in Emerson's accusation, as the quick rhythms of "Annabel Lee" testify—they're easy to parody ("Camomile Tea," "Cannibal Flea," "Bananabelly," to name a few well known parodies). But Poe I think gets the last laugh. His poems are still with us, and his idea seems right to the modern reader. He was always thinking of the sounds: besides Annabel, he gave us Lenore, Ulalume, Eulalie, and other mellifluous lovers' names.

One night the poet W. D. Snodgrass (1926-2009) came to dinner—he was born and died in January, so I've been thinking about him. He won the Pulitzer Prize for his first book, "Heart's Needle," and was our guest of honor before he was to deliver his reading at Eckerd College. But after a drink, when we sat down, Snodgrass wasn't at the table. We all looked around and then heard, from upstairs, sonorous sounds of "ommm.mm, humm.mm") rolling through the house. We soon found out he was doing his usual voice exercises. He'd determined that people "don't read poetry anymore, they just want to listen to it," and therefore decided to make his oral presentations as effective as possible. "That's where the money is," he confided. That evening his reading was great; maybe five people bought the book.

I sympathize with those who have trouble reading poetry, but I urge you to give it a try. As with everything else, you'll get better at it, and once you get the hang of it, it's addictive. And hearing poems read will help you to read them yourself. The music, the rhythms (and even the broccoli) are all in there. *Good* for you.

> *And so all the night-tide, I lie down by the side*
> *Of my darling, my darling, my life and my bride,*
>   *In her sepulcher there by the sea—*
>   *In her tomb by the side of the sea.*

  –both quotes from "Annabel Lee" by Edgar Allan Poe (1809-1849)

THE DOVE PUB

DECEMBER 24, 2015

The Sign of The Dove

... But Balthazar began to weep
foreseeing all the scenes to come:
the Child upon a darker stage
the star their spotlight stuttering out—
then shook his head smiled and sang
louder than before

Merry Christmas, everybody! I say this upfront because it's Christmas Eve, and also to gently chide those who a few years ago were shouting that our Muslim President had forbidden the use of "Merry Christmas," and we were all required to say "Season's Greetings" instead. (Donald Trump still believes it.) But "Merry Christmas" is with us yet and, like Tiny Tim, is here to stay.

We've always loved Christmas, though with our four children swooping around the world like Santa's reindeer, it's hard to organize it from one year to another. As we awaited this year's clarifications, we held long Dickensian discussions of Christmases Past. We've hung stockings in far-away places like Neuchâtel and Warsaw, in American cities like Washington DC and St. Paul, twice in Hawaii (last year with family in Kailua, and in 1993 just the two of us wandering lost on Lanai Island). But, in the spirit of "A Christmas Carol," our most memorable celebration was in 1992 in London.

During that fall we were living with 18 students in the heart of Bloomsbury. The semester was over by mid-December, and slowly our students left us and flew back home; and slowly in turn, our children began to arrive. A perk of teaching at Gower Street was that we could remain after the students left, enjoying London until the next batch, with their new professor, arrived in early January.

London is illuminated during the holidays: Big Ben, Trafalgar Square, Piccadilly Circus, the giant ferris wheel called the Eye of London, and St. Paul's Cathedral shimmer in light. We tried to imagine being in St. Paul's when John Donne was preaching: "No man is an island, entire of itself . . ." We went to plays around Leicester Square, took long walks through the parks, and listened to remarkable, not always rational, debates on soap boxes at Speakers' Corner in Hyde Park—much wittier than our recent TV political polemics. And out of many, our favorite pub was the Dove: we decided to have Christmas dinner there.

The Dove Pub is pretty perfect as pubs go—even getting there's romantic. From Goodge Street we'd take the tube to its last stop in East London. We'd walk over the Thames on the old iron and stone Hammersmith Bridge; on the right as we got off was the Riverside Theatre, where we once sat behind John Gielgud watching John Millington Singe's "Playboy of the Western World." To the left is a cluster of old buildings that include the famous designer and printer William Morris's house, and the Dove Pub, an ancient Georgian structure on the water. To get there, you have to walk through a narrow cobblestone alley (the Morris house is on the right). On the left, the pub's door leads to a small bar, its walls covered by photos of the literary and political history of London; on the right is another door leading into "the smallest barroom in England." There's a larger dining room with a big fireplace and windows looking out at the boats sculling along the Thames. At Christmas, we sat by the fire as the turkey and salmon and crisp potatoes and salad and pudding with its brandy butter rolled out, accompanied by Fuller's Ale, wines, port, and eventually brandies. Far from home, we looked around in wonder. We could see why the poet James Thomson wrote "Rule Britannia" here; toward the end of the evening, we were sure we saw Charles Dickens at another table. The Dove reeked of tradition, and our own tradition of Christmas slipped happily into it.

> *There was no dignity that night*
> *The shepherds slapped their sheepish knees*
> *and tasted too much of the grape*
> *that solaces our sober earth*
> *O blèssed be our mirth hey!*
> *Blèssed be our mirth!*

>> –both quotes from "The Gift of the Magi" by Peter Meinke, in *Liquid Paper: New & Selected Poems* (U. of Pittsburgh Press, 1991)

2016

THE EIFFEL TOWER BY TIMOTHY MEINKE, AGE 8

JANUARY 7, 2016

We'll Always Have Paris

Il pleut dans mon coeur
Comme il pleut sur la ville
Quelle est cette langueur
Qui pénétre mon coeur?

The last time we were in Paris, we stayed at the Hotel Claude Bernard on rue des Ecoles: on one corner a café, La Petite Périgourdine, and on the other side the Sorbonne, with throngs of young students. Early in our stay, after breakfast with our grown children at the café, I suggested a longish walk to the Marais district, where we could visit the Picasso Museum, inhale the calming harmony of the Place des Vosges, and enjoy one of my favorite restaurants from earlier visits, L'As du Fallafel, on the ancient rue des Rosiers.

Most streets in Paris have something interesting or beautiful to look at, and the long morning went smoothly by. But when we got to the restaurant it was packed, a line of customers stretching down the street. So were the other nearby restaurants, and after a while we started, a bit wearily, heading back toward the hotel.

We hadn't gone too far before, walking along rue Saint-Antoine, a wide avenue (compared to the narrow lanes in the Marais), we passed a small restaurant called Au Bouquet Saint Paul. It wasn't particularly distinguished-looking, but we were hungry and thirsty, so we sat down and ordered. As the wines and bread arrived, Jeanne took a few bites of her salad, looked around, and announced, "This is the best salad I've ever had in my life!"

We laugh about that—but that's exactly what Paris was to us. In large and small matters, Parisians seemed to be trying to live the good life, encouraging others to do so as well. In November, when the explosions went off (some near the Marais), our hearts sank: this was going to be Paris's 9/11 moment.

Why would any human being do such a thing? When our children were young, we took them all around the city, including the requisite visit to the Eiffel Tower, now lit up with the blue, white and red of the French flag, the motto of Paris projected on it: *Fluctuat nec Mergitur* ("Tossed by Waves but does not Sink"). We remembered the story of Jeanne's salad. "I think they're jealous," she said and, at bottom, that seems right. No matter how you cut it, *we* have a lot, and *they* don't. Paris and New York are cities that are all about finding yourself, living the good life, eating and drinking well, accepting differences, encouraging freedom of all sorts, including sexual, political, and religious. Even San Bernadino poses a threat to the enemies of difference—it's enthusiastically diverse and home to multiple consulates, including those of Guatemala and Mexico.

The jihadists are just jealous. Jealous jihadists.

Their religious fervor is a maguffin, a misleading idea sold to the maladjusted young. Some of them may believe that they're serving Allah, shouting *Allahu Akbar!* as they blow themselves and others up, but they're wrong—they don't represent Islam, and the 72 virgins won't be waiting, especially if they're in 72 pieces. The jihadists' brutality intends to terrify, but 9/11 and 12/13 didn't ruin America, and 11/13 won't ruin France. Today, the World Trade Center rises majestically over the New York skyline, crowds bustling around it as if the carnage had never happened.

Americans love to be scared by weirdo villains like Freddy Krueger and Hannibal Lecter; we know there are psychopaths out there who actually want to murder us. We've got to beat them, but not let them change our behavior.

In Paris, New York, and LA, people are gathering in their bars and cafés, taking their time, talking, debating. *Même pas peur,* they're saying: "You don't scare me." It may take a while to get back to normal; but such are the deep pleasures of freedom, as they have been and will be again.

Though for now . . .

> *It rains in my heart*
> *As it rains on the town*
> *What languor so dark*
> *That it soaks to my heart?*

> –The quotes are the first stanza from "Il Pleut dans mon Coeur" by Paul Verlaine (1844-1896). The drawing was done by Timothy Meinke when he was 8.

DONALD TRUMP

JANUARY 21, 2016

Trump

One of the low on whom assurance sits
As a silk hat on a Bradford millionaire . . .

While this will seem to some to be a weakness in myself, I couldn't help but shake my head while listening to President Obama's State of the Union address. Wouldn't anyone listening to this eloquent and generous speech, recognize that Obama is the exact opposite of Donald J. Trump in every way? The fact that millions of Americans have gone crazy about the Donald represents, if not simple racism, a massive coarsening of American education. Where is Mr. Rogers when we need him?

Recently, I received a series of right-wing "jokes" that are flooding the internet, among which were a list of "Things I Trust More than Hillary Clinton," including "OJ Simpson showing me his knife collection; an elevator ride with Ray Rice; taking pills offered by Bill Cosby; a Pakistani on a motorcycle," etc.—but the most amazing thing about them is that they're sent and believed by people eager to vote for Trump, whose lies are so large and numerous, no one keeps track anymore, not even Politifact. (I'm reminded of Mary McCarthy's remark about Lillian Hellman: "Every word she says is a lie, including 'and' and 'the'.")

I'm hoping that this is a temporary triumph (or "trumph"). Theoretically, our schools are geared to produce citizens who choose leaders for their civility, dignity, political skills, and intellectual distinction;

Trump's a stand-up comic (timing is everything), whose values mirror the bombast of popular radio and tv bloviators.

This says more about us than it does about him. He's found his audience, and it's a large one: the Republican party, whose values have spread from the Deep South to sift like lint into a mass of unappreciated, undereducated and underpaid pockets throughout the country. They believe Trump's continual braying about "political correctness." Political correctness is of course silly, but its practice is greatly overblown by people like Trump, who use this—*Tell it like it is!*—as a cover to spout racist, misogynistic, and primitive prejudices.

A while back, actor Richard Dreyfuss was in town, talking about his six years studying at Oxford University in England. From there, he said, he could clearly see how America's lack of civic education has produced a badly prepared electorate. A new Times/CBS poll shows Trump backed by 43% of Republicans with at most a high school education, by 28% with bachelor degrees, and by 21% with some graduate study. Our high schools used to be terrific, but this is a worrying trend: the less educated one is the more likely he or she will choose candidates like Trump.

Trump's not only still around but, by recognizing the sullen resentment sprouting like mushrooms in the GOP's back yard, has bent the whole party's direction. He's not just a "jerk," as Jeb Bush called him, but the man on a very white horse that the party's been waiting for. He'll save them from those funny-looking newcomers whose children are winning all the prizes in school and then take the best-paying jobs away from them.

The longing for this kind of hero has been building for decades, gathering speed with the election of George W. Bush, always proud of pronouncing "nuclear" as "nucular": *In your face, pointy-headed intellectuals!* A clearer warning flag was hoisted in 2008 with the party's jubilant embrace of Sarah Palin, a non-reader who flaunted her ignorance—and they loved her for it.

Well, Welcome Donald! I have confidence in the wisdom of the American majority. Bring him on! He's HUGE, patriotic and conservative, a combination of Archie Bunker and John Wayne (both lovable!), keeping women, gays and blacks in their proper places. Let's nominate the rascal and bring on the debate!

Still, I'm worried—occasionally I wake up at night thinking, Who'd have believed an educated Christian country would ever elect a failed artist who was a high school dropout with a bona fide inferiority complex?

> *Shall I at least set my lands in order?*
> *London Bridge is falling down falling down falling down...*

–both quotes from "The Waste Land" by T.S. Eliot (1888-1965)

THEATRE TICKETS

FEBRUARY 4, 2016

All the World's a Stage

You've got to be taught
To hate and fear,
You've got to be taught
From year to year,
It's got to be drummed
In your dear little ear . . .

In 1949, for my 17th birthday, my parents changed my life. They took me to see "South Pacific," the Rodgers and Hammerstein musical that had opened on Broadway earlier that year. Mary Martin sang the part of nurse Nellie Forbush, and a 58-year-old opera singer, Ezio Pinza, became an unlikely American hero as the French plantation owner, Emile DeBacque. Based on James Michener's Pulitzer-Prize-winning collection of 19 short stories, the music, the acting, and the words knocked my scruffy argyles off.

There's nothing like real theatre (although, as one of the songs tells us, "There's nothing like a dame," either). Jeanne and I are movie fans, too, but the vulnerability of real actors on a stage gives theatre an extra intensity compared to the distancing permanence of film. "South Pacific" was the first play I'd seen outside of high school, and I was hooked. (If someone had told me that 40 years later James Michener would have dinner at our house, I would've fainted. In 1990, still a fierce liberal at 83, Michener was a popular and gracious "helper" in Eckerd's fiction-writing classes for a semester.)

Theatre, especially in big cities, can be expensive, so Jeanne and

I limit our New York theatre visits to one yearly splurge, last year seeing a quietly moving play, "The Weir," by the Irish playwright Conor McPherson. This reminded us of the first NYC production we saw together, in 1958, a year after we were married: another Irish play, "Brendon Behan's "The Hostage," about the Irish civil war, which takes place in a very weird brothel. We'll never forget the end when the "hero," a young British soldier who's just been killed, jumps out of his coffin and sings "O death where is thy sting-a-ling-a-ling?"

A different kind of transcendent conclusion came when we saw Ibsen's "Ghosts" in an off-Broadway production. It was a theatre-in-the round production, and we had seats on an aisle about half-way from the stage. In the end, when Mrs. Alving's son died, she—played by the great Irish actress Siobhan McKenna—staggered off the stage and down the aisle, weeping inconsolably the whole way, right past us. We wanted to reach out and comfort her. We thought, this was a matinee, and McKenna would have to repeat this agonized performance in a few hours. Actors have to be tough.

Even in other languages, theatre works its magic. When we saw "Hamlet" in Warsaw, performed in Polish, it was still powerful, even though we hardly understood a word, barely recognizing *"Być albo nie być"* ("To be or not to be . . ."). But "Hamlet" on stage can even transcend Shakespeare's poetry. The sword-fights helped.

In "South Pacific," great songs abounded: "Some Enchanted Evening," "Bali Ha'i," "Younger Than Springtime," "Bloody Mary," and others, but the one I learned by heart was "Carefully Taught." In 1949, as a senior in an all-white high school who'd never thought much about race, it struck me immediately as beautiful and true. And in today's vitriolic political climate, it still speaks right to the point.

Over the decades, we've been lucky to live here as the Tampa Bay theatre scene has blossomed. We love theatre because it's physical and moving. But, as in the two plays on stage in St. Pete right now—August Wilson's "Jitney" at American Stage and Thornton Wilder's

"Our Town," at FreeFall—it can also show us America from the inside, not as a lesson or a lecture, but how it's actually lived.

"All the world's a stage," the bard tells us. Let's do our part: support our actors and get those tickets.

> *You've got to be taught before it's too late,*
> *Before you are six or seven or eight,*
> *To hate all the people your relatives hate,*
> *You've got to be carefully taught.*
>
> –both quotes from "Carefully Taught," by Rodgers and Hammerstein in "South Pacific," 1948.

MRS. VANDERBILT

FEBRUARY 18, 2016

Maureen Vanderbilt

What do we want from our friends if not a
lifting once in a while of the world's weight:
I see you hunched at your desk eyes inches
from a book . . .

The poet Josephine Jacobsen once said, "Poetry is an immensely private occupation"; she'd never think of showing a poem to anyone before it was finished. I've lived my "poetic life," such as it is, in the Jacobsen camp, keeping my poems to myself until I feel they're ready to send to an editor. I'd never taken a Writing Workshop, so when I went to grad school after the Army, I took the literary Ph. D. route to become a college teacher, support my family, and have "lots of time to write," a proposition Politifact would rate "Pants on Fire."

MFA degrees were just coming into existence. I occasionally visited the University of Michigan's Creative Writing program, but was too shy and busy to make friends or find mentors; I did go to the readings there, and studied the poems of its teachers (Donald Hall, Radcliffe Squires, X. J. Kennedy, and others were at Michigan in 1960). I was taking classes in Beowulf, Chaucer, the Renaissance, 19th Century Russian Literature, and Art History. That was a good education, and with my M.A. degree, I got a job teaching Freshman English at Hamline University in St. Paul, finishing the Ph. D. at Minnesota.

Still, like almost every writer I know, I did have important encouragement from teachers when I was young. One of them, in a specific and vivid moment, gave me an early push and brightened the path. Poets don't need a lot of encouragement, but they need some.

In little Mountain Lakes High School, New Jersey, we had an outstanding teacher named Mrs. Maureen Vanderbilt (in the 1940's, with almost all other venues closed to them, brilliant women wound up teaching school for pennies). One morning she surprised us with a quiz on the essays of Charles Lamb, which I hadn't read (I seldom read assignments, preferring my mother's bodice-ripping Book-of-the Month Club novels for night-time reading—forbidden, of course). Hoping she'd let me off the hook for my cleverness, I wrote *I dislike Lamb / In fact I shun him / As to his essays / I haven't done 'em*, and turned it in. When the papers came back the next day, she had written in her precise hand, *You have my sympathy / For your antipathy / But there'll be Lamb / On your exam*—followed by a small but very distinct "F." As soon as I got over the shock of the "F," I began to nod my head: This was more like it. Here was the kind of relationship I—a closeted poet—had been looking for. For the next year, a fountain of poetry poured out, much of which I attached to her papers (though I became more careful with my homework). When my high school yearbook came out, she was its advisor, and despite my being basically still a secret poet, the Yearbook read: *Peter Meinke. Wants to be: Writer. Probably will be: Censored.*

Looking for a mentor is a normal impulse. Even the agoraphobic Emily Dickinson asked advice of strangers like the editor Thomas Wentworth Higginson, which of course she never followed. From the coffee houses of London to the cafés of Paris to the MFA programs of American universities, writers young and old have always searched for guidance and friendship from talented and like-minded contemporaries. There are many ways to get and use (or not use) advice. Our job, as writers and artists, is to find the right way for ourselves.

*. . . remembering
not only how you were funny but how
you made us realize
though the best things happen outside of books
books too are vital our best words and thoughts
pooling on paper . . .*

−both quotes from "The Teacher" by Peter Meinke, in *Zinc Fingers* (U. of Pittsburgh Press, 2000).

SENATOR TED CRUZ

MARCH 3, 2016

Stampeding Elephants

'Tis education forms the common mind,
Just as the twig is bent, the tree's inclin'd.

In an article on Donald Trump, I suggested that a coarsening of our educational system has resulted in a rash of citizens falling for blatant fear-baiting rhetoric bereft of both facts and common sense. Obviously, this tactic has been around forever—but there's a definite increase in both those who spout doomsday rhetoric and those who believe it.

Real education's taking a back seat. Where is skepticism, or even normal curiosity? Hordes of speakers have parroted the phrase, "job-killing Obamacare" for years, not in the least slowed down by our country's unemployment numbers steadily falling to 5% (Romney promised to get down to 6%, and his audiences cheered wildly). The fact that jobs don't pay as much as they used to is another subject—automation, outsourcing, the collapse of unions—unconnected to the Affordable Care Act.

It's not just Trump, though right now, with the help of the media, he's making the most noise. Now that he's been "winning, winning," as Cokey Roberts observed, "he's not so funny anymore." But Senator Ted Cruz is less funny and more scary. With his "carpet bombing till the sands glow" threats, he sounds more like North Korea's Kim Jong-un wiggling his nuclear trigger finger than someone who claims to have "a personal relationship with Jesus Christ." This, too, brings enormous applause, so my thought is, Do they understand what he's saying? And if so, Do they really want him for President?

In a recent letter to Editor David Warner, a reader named John attacked me for some "anti-Trump" remarks I'd written (though I was quoting Republican criticisms). John's clearest sentence went as follows: "The reason this country is in such decline is because of all the left wing teachers in this country are [sic] indoctrinating the youth into your wacko ideology which has been proven time and time again to be a complete failure."

Well, no details are given, but he seems to be talking about the wacko ideology that brought us Social Security, Medicare, Health Care, Fair Labor Standards (including the banning of child labor), Civil Rights Law, Gay Rights decisions, and Climate Change awareness. There are other laws I'd guess he wouldn't like, but it's hard to say, because all he tells us is that the "ideology" is something that's been proved "time and time again" to be a total bust.

Is he talking about Germany? Norway? France? We're clearly doing better than they are these days, thanks to President Obama's "ideologies," though they remain charming countries to visit. It's true that most—by no means all— college teachers are on the left, but that's natural: They read more. They speak more languages. They believe in Climate Change. It's hard to figure where John's overstated and overheated vitriol comes from.

Maybe he's been bullied by thugs with accents. He thinks Obama's a Muslim and Clinton's a Nazi, but I'd gently urge him to check Wikipedia or Politifact or just get out a bit more. I don't know if John has lost his wife or his wallet, his job or his mind. If any of these dire things are true, and this isn't just a snit, trust me, John, both President Obama and I wish you better luck.

It sounds to me that he's picked up the frumious tone of Senator Cruz, our own Bandersnatch (via Lewis Carroll), who's coldly racing Trump to scoop up the "angry vote." In my article I implied the acceptance of crazy ideas and general name-calling—even Marco Rubio has joined in now—might be attributable to faulty information pooling in our schools and living rooms. Bad manners breed in stagnant water like zika-bearing mosquitoes.

Uh-oh, I've just been bitten, so I'll join John and the others, and end with a quote from one of my favorite authors:

> *Sir, I admit your gen'ral rule*
> *That every poet is a fool;*
> *But you yourself may serve to show it,*
> *That every fool is not a poet.*

> –"Epigram from the French" and (above) from "Epistles to Several Persons," by Alexander Pope (1688-1744).

FOUR-LEAF CLOVER

MARCH 17, 2016

Luck of the Irish

You were silly like us, your gift survived us all:
The parish of rich women, physical decay,
Yourself. Mad Ireland hurt you into poetry . . .

My mother was Kathleen McDonald, whose father, James McDonald, came over from County Louth (the "wee" county) in Ireland, to work, not too happily, as a postman in Brooklyn. As long as I can remember, St. Patrick's Day has been a party featuring green clothing and brown drinks (e.g., Guinness and whiskey), and Jeanne and I follow the tradition to this day, including notes or phone calls to faraway Irish friends to reminisce about parties past.

The whole family enjoyed these convivial festivities. Although my dad, Harry Meinke, came from stoic German stock he enjoyed any holiday that included extra drinks, so was happy to join in the annual St. Patty's Day party. And Jeanne's family branches from ancient Welsh/English stock: close enough, we figure, to qualify for an Irish celebration.

As children we often heard the phrase, the "luck of the Irish," and were told this luck could be augmented by finding a four-leaf clover. This resulted in my sisters and me spending hours scouring the tiny lawns in our Flatbush neighborhood. There wasn't a lot of greenery on our block, so we would head on occasion to nearby Marine Park where there was at least some grass, and—believe it or not—we did find the occasional lucky prize. I had a couple of them pressed into a book that somehow didn't survive our various moves. (*Bad luck!*) Of course, as we grew older we realized we were sent on our clover hunts just to get us out of the house and out of the way (there wasn't much talk about the real Irish symbol, the clover-like shamrock). But we grew up believing we had the luck of the Irish, and Jeanne, who believes more that we have a "guardian angel," saw that these beliefs easily meshed together.

We sit in our house and look out at the flowers and trees on our small lot, and think, Aren't we lucky! We can trace our being here through a series of lucky accidents. I like to say we're here because of Bertolt Brecht. When we moved to St. Paul, Hamline University randomly picked us to live in a house where Jim Carlson, a theatre professor, lived upstairs. In the early 1960's Jim put on the American premiers of several of Brecht's greatest plays, like "Mother Courage" and "The Good Person of Szechwan" (Jim had studied at the University of Minnesota under Eric Bentley, Brecht's translator). Called into the president's office, Jim thought he was being promoted to be Director of the Theatre, at last—but the president looked at him and said, "Why are you putting on all these Communist plays?" This was the '60's, remember.

This led to a string of "lucky accidents," and Jim wound up founding the theatre for a new and radical school (No grades! Independent study! Overseas classes!) named Florida Presbyterian College, whose new dean was a great fan of a small rule-breaking magazine, *motive*, where I was publishing many of my early poems (just because Jim had a subscription to it).

Of course, the "luck of the Irish" has always been a two-edged sword. As one of my tougher Brooklyn aunts once said, "Some guy goes walking and steps in dog poop, and someone else says, 'Lucky you had your shoes on!' Well, that's the luck of the Irish." (We found the same dark humor the year we lived in Poland. Next New Year's

Eve they'll lift their vodkas, look in your eyes, and say "May 2016 be worse than 2017.")

Well, although over the long years the families did have their share of problems, I can still hear our mother playing the piano, and Dad and our favorite uncle, my mother's alcoholic golden-voiced brother, singing their hearts out at those St. Patrick's Day parties; and I think we were pretty lucky.

> *Follow, poet, follow right*
> *To the bottom of the night,*
> *With your unconstraining voice*
> *Still persuade us to rejoice.*

> –both quotes from "In Memory of W. B. Yeats" by W. H. Auden (1907-1973)

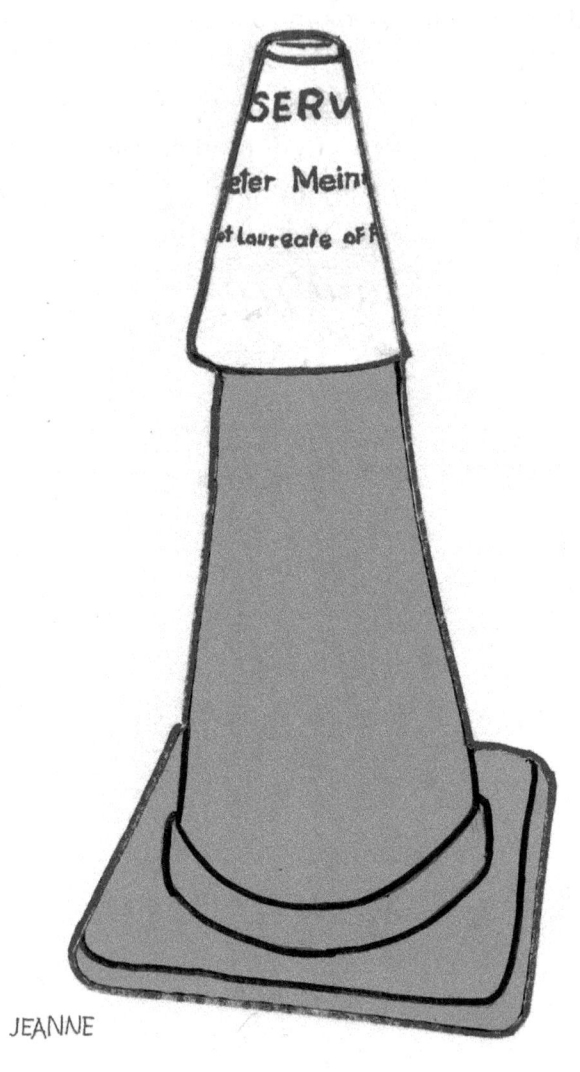

PARKING CONE AT GULFPORT LIBRARY

MARCH 31, 2016

Assuming the Position

I have started to say
'A quarter of a century'
Or 'thirty years back'
About my own life . . .

When we arrived at the Hickman Theatre in Gulfport for a reading a while ago, we circled around the crowded parking lot for a few minutes before spotting the Laureate Parking Cone. *Now there's a perk*, we agreed. "I oughta swipe it," Jeanne said, using her criminal voice. "Who's gonna bust the wife of the Poet Laureate?"

Regrettably, we didn't pinch it, but we sometimes pinch ourselves as we move steadily through the months on the Laureate carousel. Already National Poetry Month is upon us, time to give what may be (for two more years) our annual report.

Hearing that I might be anointed Poet Laureate of Florida, an old friend wrote to say, "Peter, while you're considering, I hope you'll remember this letter," attaching some comments that British poet Philip Larkin wrote when declining both the Oxford Professorship of Poetry (in 1968) and the country's Poet Laureateship (in 1984), England's two highest poetry positions.

Basically, Larkin claimed that he was "unfitted" for these roles, because he wasn't good at talking about poetry, and in addition, his view of "hell on earth" was a literary party drinking "washing sherry" with people he didn't want to know. He had the uncanny ability to say things you don't agree with that hold an unsettling degree of truth.

Larkin's brilliant and often funny poems combine an intense fear of death with a Swiftian disgust for life. Though he had his share of friends and lovers he was a bachelor and librarian all his days, which shows that he knew himself pretty well. I, on the other hand, taught poetry for over 30 years, and have been married to Jeanne for 58 (raising 4 inquisitive children), so am somewhat accustomed to confusing real-life activity. Still, I agree with Larkin's basic point: The main job of a poet should be to write poetry, not analyze or sell it. (I'm not comparing myself to a great poet like Larkin, but as a person; for example, I'm not too fussy about sherry.)

I resist the poet-in-a-garret stereotype, preferring the poet-as-citizen group (along with Juan Felipe Herrera, America's Poet Laureate who gave a delightful reading at the Palladium recently). I like the idea of wandering around Florida's schools and libraries reading poems, hoping a few might take root in someone's heart or mind, bringing pleasure and thoughtfulness that can be shared.

The upshot, of course, is that I said Yes, so we're busier than we ever thought we'd be at our ages, giving readings throughout the state to big and little (not to say miniscule) audiences. Add to this the enormous weight of weighing every word and line in our bi-weekly *Poet's Notebook* columns and drawings, plus trying to keep up the writing that resulted in my being chosen in the first place, you can see why we often feel a bit stretched. Fortunately, this is driving me to drink; just part of the job.

Two Larkinesque questions emerge: 1) How much time will be left to write more poems; and 2) Given the fact that most poets' best work is done when they're young, is it worth it? Well, like most questions concerning poetry, there are no real answers (there are no real answers to many important questions: *What is life? Why is it so hard to read menus?*).

I believe in the magic of poems; and am happy and proud to be Florida's Johnny Appleseed of poetry, dropping my applepoems semi-randomly around a State that leans toward oranges. Although part of the poet's job is to "speak truth to power" (read *Poet's Notebook*), poetry's basic nature is to celebrate the wonder of life, and make people happier. For three years, I'll try to do this.

All that's left to happen
Is some deaths (my own included).
Their order, and their manner,
Remain to be learnt.

 –both quotes from "I have started to say" by Philip Larkin (1922-1985), from *Collected Poems*, Farrar, Straus & Giroux , 1988

YBOR TROLLEY STOP WITH CHAIRS

APRIL 14, 2016

Ybor City

They let women work
in the factories
at the hardest job:
Stripping the brittle stems
from tobacco leaves because
our fingers were nimble
and we'd take less pay...

Bending over the long bench
we smiled to ourselves
because we were helping
the children grow free...

and in the end
what do we love?
Freedom Family!

    The above poem is engraved on a chair at the 13th Street and 7th Avenue trolley stop in Ybor City. (In Jeanne's drawing, you can see the engraved plaques at the tops of the chairs.) Poet Sylvia Curbelo and I were commissioned to write short poems about Ybor's female cigar makers, to be fastened onto bronze replicas of their chairs and scattered around trolley stops in English, Italian, and Spanish. It's a sort of street level art, like historic drinking fountains in a park, or murals on an alley wall, maybe hard to find but fun when you see it. Jeanne and I once walked around New York looking for

Keith Haring's surreal public art, one of which we found in the Men's Room at an LBGT Community Center in Greenwich Village.

In what would have been more noticeable, a while back St. Pete hired artists Carol Mickett and Bob Stackhouse to design lovely and functional bus stops along Central Avenue, and we're very disappointed that this seems to have been derailed. The Mickett/Stackhouse duo is justifiably famous, and would have been another international feather in the city's art cap, like Chihuly and Dali.

In a civilized world—in any world—art should play a central role in the ordinary lives of its citizens. Many of the pleasures of touring Europe are found not just in Paris, London, or Rome, but in the towns, villages and hamlets, with charming and even stunning fountains, statues, churches, and cafés. In Neuchâtel, Switzerland, the trolleys, like Ybor's, were picturesque, and the stops (from the train station and around the town) were at lively destinations—markets, bistros, schools, theatres, museums, pools, and ice rinks.

Ybor City reminds us of Europe in general, not just Cuba and Spain. (How good that we'll be able to fly to Cuba soon!) Its rich history, integrated architecture, ethnic restaurants, and reputation for a high-spirited night life drew us over the Bay right away when we arrived here in 1966. The appeal was similar to those other risqué evening playgrounds like Paris's Montmartre, London's Soho, New York's Greenwich Village, New Orlean's Bourbon Street, and Florida's own Key West. These towns and districts are like living works of art, offering strings of surprises popping off like Chinese firecrackers. What defines a place as "arty" is always an over-all effect brought on by a multitude of stimuli.

Our first real encounter with Ybor was through music and poetry. I gave a reading in one of the night clubs—I forget the name—alternating with a small and lively band. I soon found myself sitting at the bar with the talented young pianist and band leader, Paul Wilborn. In the years to come, he became Tampa's "Art Czar" under

Mayor Pam Ioro, and then later moved to St. Pete to become Palladium Paul. He and his wife, the singer/actor Eugenie Bonderant (recently seen as Tigris in "Hunger Games: Mockingjay Part 2") are now our neighbors in South St. Pete.

I'm grateful to be connected with Ybor, and enjoyed writing about those cigar-making women getting through their long days by listening to the lectors read the day's news, essays, stories, novels, and even some serious poetry to pull them through the hours. Producing a democratic ideal—a disciplined, intelligent, and informed working class—this had to be better than what we find on TV today.

One last thing, a little embarrassing, but to my ear the end of my poem sounds more dramatic in Italian than English:

> *ed alla fine*
> *che cosa amiamo?*
> *Libertà Famiglia!*

>   –both quotes from "Women at Work" ("La Donne al Lavoro") by Peter Meinke (2000)

MORNING COFFEE

APRIL 28, 2016

Drinking Cooperation

Amelia dreams she's a child
chided for daydreaming.

Amelia!
Amelia Earhart!

Keep your head out of the clouds
and your feet on the ground...

As we near Mother's Day, and Hillary Clinton moves closer to her destination, I'm finally hearing some conversations about what's been missing from her campaign, *i.e.*, her most obvious attribute: she's a woman.

Of course, she can't talk about it, any more than President Obama can talk about being black. Anything they can say about their gender or race can be twisted in too many "self-serving" directions. A President has to represent everyone equally. Many blacks feel that Obama's bent over backwards not to show favoritism, and are disappointed with his lack of support. With Clinton, it's even more complicated; it has to do with *femaleness*: what a woman president would mean for this country.

Google recently did a study on what makes some workplaces more efficient than others, and came up with "psychological safety." People perform together effectively in workplaces that reaffirm them emotionally; and, it observed, women create those kinds of atmospheres far better than men, who still tend to play "King of the Hill."

This sounds true to my experience. I'm no expert: when I write a poem or a story from the point of view of a woman, I simply have her think the same way I do, subtracting football. There must be better ways to do this. But it's clear that there are many more women on the poetry scene today than there were in the 1950's, and the atmosphere is healthier, less cutthroat, more fun. Better yet, the poetry's wonderful (just recently in Florida, Tampa's Erica Dawson won the prestigious Poet's Prize, Helen Wallace was appointed Poet Laureate of St. Petersburg, Tallahassee's Brandi George won Florida's Gold Medal in Poetry, and Miami's Denise Duhamel delighted a crowd at the Dali Museum).

In other fields, women are doing the work traditionally assigned to men—and performing well. Janet Yellen leads the Fed more gently and thoughtfully than Ben Bernanke; and our economy's pulling out of the recession. Angela Merkel is holding the European Union together with her generosity and efficiency; in a long article in the New York Times, Daniel Kehlmann observed that Merkel's "risky compassion" for the desperate and suffering immigrants may "cost her the chancellorship, but at the same time save Germany's soul." Long before Pope Francis, America's "nuns on the bus" have been humanizing the Catholic Church's stern patriarchy. And soon, Harriet Tubman, "Conductor on the Underground Railway," will represent America on the 20 dollar bill far better than Andrew Jackson (although I was hoping for Emily Dickinson).

Women bring more fully human values to their jobs. It's telling that two famous female Prime Ministers of a few generations ago, Margaret Thatcher (England) and Golda Meir (Israel) were both nicknamed "the Iron Lady"—serving in a male-dominated workplace, they ruled it with "male" force. Today's women, as their numbers in the workforce rise, seem more confident in their own cooperative instincts. In her roles as New York Senator and Secretary of State, Clinton was known for her pragmatic compromising (today's do-nothing Congress shows us what a lack of that skill can bring about). This of course isn't as romantic as Bernie's one-note crusade—but it works.

Everyone wants to talk about Clinton's "email problem"—an issue that will go nowhere. Republicans have long been "Swiftboating" Clinton—whose statements are rated by Politifact as 95% True or Mostly True, miles better than anyone else—on the honesty question. Call her email handling anything you want (stupid, silly, careless), but she can be trusted on women's rights, climate change, health care, gun law; she's changed her mind on some things, as she should, but she'll be careful and she's experienced; and she's a woman.

Our world hasn't used women well. We should recognize this, and drink cooperation with our morning coffee, as Jeanne's drawing suggests. Sometimes, of course, I add a wee bit of something else to mine.

Amelia turns
and giggles in her sleep.

–both quotes from "Night Flights: Amelia Earhart's Dreams" by Linda Eve Diamond, Aventine Press 2013

AZALEA PHOTO BY JEANNE

MAY 12, 2016

The Bibliophiles

I never met a library I didn't like.
    –William Stafford in "The Art of Poetry," Paris Review, issue # 67.

Recently I was invited to read at the Seminole Community Library to the Florida Bibliophile Society. That was a fine combination: Poets (well, all writers, I suppose) love libraries; when I see a book of mine in a library, I think, "Good; you've found a home." And bibliophiles—people who love and collect books—are by definition friends of ours. At the end of the reading they gave me a present that suggested they were clairvoyant as well.

The gift was a small but handsome hardcover book, "A Wordsworth Anthology"—an unexpected trifecta of sorts. First, not only do I love many of Wordsworth's poems, but—as I've written here before—visiting his home in England's Lake District led Jeanne and me to move into our tree-covered cottage and fill our yard with the azaleas that enrich our lives every day (see Jeanne's photo).

The second bonus of the *Anthology* is its long introduction by Laurence Housman. I remembered his name immediately: he founded England's most "radical and progressive" book store, Housmans Bookshop in King's Cross, London, not far from where we lived with Eckerd students on Gower Street. I'm happy to say it's still going strong: recently it held a reading/signing of *Royal Babylon; The Case Against the Monarchy*, a prose-poem by Heathcote Williams. In today's fractious political atmosphere, America could use more book stores like this.

Housman was the younger brother of poet A. E. Housman (1859-1936), the author of *A Shropshire Lad*, with its memorable lines, among others, "Oh many a peer of England brews / Livelier liquor than the Muse, / And malt does more than Milton can / To justify God's way to man." Although he (Laurence) gives Wordsworth great praise, his wit is reminiscent of his older brother's when he criticizes the poet's late conservatism, singling out a sonnet sequence defending capital punishment ("Sonnets Upon the Punishment of Death") which "tends to make you dislike God and man about equally."

But the biggest surprise of the *Anthology* was its origin. It's from the estate of one of my favorite poets, William Stafford (1914-1993)—Oregon's long-term Poet Laureate and in 1970 the Poetry Consultant to the Library of Congress—inscribed to him by John Gross, his roommate at the Iowa Writing Workshop. Stafford's most famous poem is "Traveling Through the Dark," about meeting a pregnant dead deer on a dangerous curve. But he was equally famous for his amazing work habits, getting up in the dark every morning, writing thousands of poems that resulted in 57 books!

I saw these habits the first time I met him, at a Poetry Festival in Abingdon, Va., where we were scheduled to read. The night we arrived we stayed up late at the hotel bar, chatting about mutual friends and politics (he was a conscientious objector in World War II—we had lots to talk about). At 8 a.m., I staggered down to breakfast (we were on a panel at 9), and there was Bill, polishing up a poem he had already written about a meeting with the night watchman. "I have wasted my life," I said to him, quoting a line from James Wright and shaking my aching head.

At the panel, Stafford told the students that a writer's job was to "write day in and day out, no matter what happens." A student asked,

"Mr. Stafford, do you really write every single morning?" "I do," Bill said. "But"—the student persisted—"what if you can't think of anything?" Bill thought a moment, as if he were giving his answer for the first time. "Well," he said, "I lower my standards."

So thanks again to the Bibliophiles for their thoughtful gift full of rich and resonant memories.

> *Dwarves and Giants, Pinkshell, Flame—*
> *O my dear, so many azaleas are dying!*
> *We must have a party! Here! This afternoon!*
>
> –from "Azaleas" by Peter Meinke, in *Liquid Paper: New & Selected Poems*, U. of Pittsburgh Press 1991

BASEBALL PITCHER

MAY 19, 2016

Baseball: The Fan Problem

Yesterday I was told
the trouble with America is that
these kids here
would rather be DiMaggio
than Byron: this shows our decadence
But I don't know
there's not that much difference
Byron also would have married Monroe
or at least been in there trying . . .

The Rays got off to a slow start this season, and I surprised myself by giving a fig, having long ago weaned myself from caring about the fates of grown men getting overpaid for whacking a little ball. But the team was struggling so valiantly—with the shaky fate of their stadium, the departure of tainted Manny, losing their first six games, poor attendance—I felt an affection for them not experienced since I was a young baseball fan in Brooklyn. So I was happy when they started to turn around and play some exciting ball, like last year's team. I hope the attendance turns around, too, but it's hard to be optimistic.

On our walk this morning, Jeanne—who up to then had hidden any deep interest in baseball—said it's obvious why Rays fans get outnumbered even in their home park. "No one who lives here is *from* here," she pointed out. "And you're the same, still moping about the Dodgers leaving for California a hundred years ago."

Well, I'm not that old. It was just 1957, and when the team moved to Los Angeles, like the Pied Piper it led the Giants out of the Polo Grounds to San Francisco, leaving the Yankees behind to gobble up all those fans. But Jeanne's right: the difference between L.A., San Francisco, and Tampa Bay is that the first two aren't populated by snowbirds from Chicago (*Go Cubs!*), Detroit (*Yay Tigers!*), and Minneapolis (*Rock'em Twins!*), not to mention the Yankee fans, who outnumber everyone else, especially if you add in anti-Yankee fans, who attend games to root *against* them, like a juiced-up battery with plus and minus poles.

The fan problem with the Rays is similar to the problem faced by the "financially troubled" Florida Orchestra (they're both on the low salary edge of their professions, though the musicians get paid a heap less than the ballplayers): they've got a small solid base, but how can they hook the youngsters into becoming regular paying customers?

With the Orchestra, in these tough economic times, the prevalence of white hair in the audience makes one think they could just reverse the usual practice of "senior discounts" and give everyone under 60 a "junior discount." With the Rays, it's a bit more complicated.

In Brooklyn, every boy played baseball—or the city substitute, stickball—in the streets, swinging broomsticks at a rubber ball, very good for developing hand-eye coordination, as Willie Mays testified. But now young people, boys and girls, play and follow soccer, tennis, basketball, and even golf: this is a good thing, except for a young baseball team trying to build a fan base. The only real hope might be to get the kids to watch baseball on TV, where they're apparently glued for about 30 hours per week anyway.

And maybe, if they could just hop on a tram or a train to the stadium, they would come. Governor Scott, are you listening?

And on the other hand you

have to admit that DiMag played
sweet music
out there in the magic grass
of centerfield

    –both quotes from "Byron vs. DiMaggio" by Peter Meinke, in *Liquid Paper*, 1991)

Peter Meinke still has his old glove which, like his hands, is cracking like a withered leaf.

BICYCLE PLAYING CARDS

MAY 26, 2016

The Cost of War

Read 'em and weep.

–Old poker expression heard a lot in the Army

When I finished my time as a draftee, I was sent home from Germany by slow military ship. The hold below decks was crammed with hammock-like double-bunks, which quickly developed a permanent sour stench from seasick soldiers vomiting over the bunks and each other. To get out of this unhealthy air a friend of mine and I—going against the old Army rule of never volunteering for anything—volunteered to work for the chaplain, whose office was higher up on the ship. Lying our sinful heads off about our knowledge of the Protestant, Catholic and Jewish rituals available on board (in 1957, the idea that Muslims existed hadn't occurred to anyone connected to the Chaplain's office), we were hired by a very bored officer. As far as I can remember, no one ever checked up on us, or even came by to worship.

We had in fact very little to do, so our "job" soon morphed into distributing toys and games to the children of the officers who were accompanying us privates and pfc's home. There weren't too many children, but we had a world-class hoard of board games like Monopoly, Parcheesi, chess, checkers, Chinese checkers, cribbage, and uncountable decks of cards, many of them the handsome oversized Bicycle variety. Greg (my fellow dungeon-dodger) and I sat in a small room with a sliding interior window and, after reading up on the rules, played endless hours of cribbage, checking out various items to the children, who were supposed to return them at the end of the day. (We also could duck up a small stairwell for fresh air, which we did sparingly, not wanting to get questioned and sent back below.) In this way we spent our sea-going week in a reasonably comfortable and pleasant way.

As we neared home, we asked the Chaplain where we should stack these treasures, especially those that were scratched or damaged. To our surprise, we were told to throw them all out: damaged, used, or untouched. We'd long ago learned not to question orders, just pretend we understood. Obviously, it was easier for them to order new games each year. Although Greg and I were happy to obey—it meant more time outside—we returning privates (earning $98 a month) thought it an enormous waste of money, tossing perfectly good games into the Harbor under the fixed copper stare of the Statue of Liberty, even though we distributed decks of cards to our fellow draftees, and smuggled out a few sets of cribbage for ourselves.

I remembered this minor crime when I read recently that our military has wasted at least 8.5 trillion dollars in taxpayer money since 1996.

We know there are millions of Americans suffering from poverty, even hunger. We know we have an oddly connected obesity problem—the poor are fatter—and we don't live as long as we should. Our racial wounds are still open, and our sexual prejudices still harmful. Our infrastructure's inadequate and crumbling. Almost every city, including ours, seems to be having a homeless crisis. Public education's in turmoil.

And each year we spend 600.4 billion dollars on the military (2013 figures). That's more than the next nine countries, friend or foe, combined.

Shouldn't we know that this is just plain crazy?

We could cut 400 billion from that bill and still be able to chant,

"We're #1! We're #1!" China, next in line, spends a paltry $112.2 billion on their "defense."

Has this gargantuan expenditure on soldiers and guns made us feel happy, or at least safe? Apparently not. Some Americans think we kill too many people; some think we don't kill enough. America's very upset. But are they yelling about that 600 billion dollar number?

What's that? Speak up!

A Dead Statesman

I could not dig: I dared not rob:
Therefore I lied to please the mob.
Now all my lies are proved untrue
And I must face the men I slew
What tale shall serve me here among
Mine angry and defrauded young?

–from "Epitaphs of War" by Rudyard Kipling (1865-1936)

W. B. YEATS' GRAVE

JUNE 9, 2016

William Butler Yeats

Cast a cold eye
On life, on death.
Horseman, pass by.

–lines (from "Under Ben Bulben") on W. B. Yeats's gravestone

On November 3rd, 1992, while America was spreading its votes among three presidential candidates, Jeanne and I were standing in a brooding cemetery in Sligo, Ireland. Our thoughts were far from the noisy battle between George H. W. Bush, Ross Perot, and Bill Clinton, an election that would change American politics for years to come (and is still affecting us today). But we were thinking more serious thoughts: we were reading the above words cut in stone at the grave of the 20th Century's greatest poet: William Butler Yeats. A cold wind was blowing; it was getting dark and no one else was in the churchyard. I half-whispered his poem, "The Lake Isle of Innisfree," (the lake just west of us, in Sligo County, where Yeats spent his childhood), thinking of his shaky old voice reciting it, on the only recording I have of him. Then Jeanne took this photo and we hiked up the highway toward the lights of a lone pub, and waited for the bus back to town.

A question I often get asked is, "Who's your favorite poet?," and I tend to give different answers, which is truthful enough, as my mind changes from age to age, and even season to season. Probably, like a favorite song, or a favorite meal, we just need some diversity along the line.

But a good test for this question might be, "Which poems do you commit to memory?" Memorizing poetry takes time and dedication; in short, a long-term relationship. I thought of this when I turned the calendar and saw that June 13th was Yeats's birthday; we'll lift a Smithwick's Irish Ale to him next Monday, but no candles: Yeats (1865-1939) will be 151.

Over the years I memorized hundreds of poems, and many of them stayed operative in my mind through the decades when I was a teacher, and had reasons to say them out loud. These days, like our old friends, there are fewer remaining (I'm talking about whole poems, not bits and snatches), but as I lie in bed rolling them through my head and waiting for sleep, I see that there are more poems by Yeats than anyone else, including Shakespeare (in second place). Besides "The Lake Isle," I love to say, or think, "The Second Coming," "Who Goes with Fergus?," "The Song of Wandering Aengus," "Down By the Salley Gardens," and a few others whose titles I'm blanking on right now. The poems I love are falling from me like the leaves over our garden.

My students were generally displeased when I made them memorize poems—"Learn them by heart," I'd tell them, emphasizing *heart*—though a fair number have written back to say how much they enjoy the ones they've kept in their noggins. Many of my writing students memorized their own poems, ones they wrote themselves; and I said that was fine, and could help you at readings—-but memorizing other writers' poems is much better for you as a writer, adding the rhythms and thought processes from the poets you love and admire. This can only help your own poems, giving your voice a richness and complexity it would otherwise lack.

The stanza that precedes the words written on Yeats's tombstone begins "Under bare Ben Bulben's head / In Drumcliff churchyard

Yeats is laid . . ." In the epitaph I wrote for a contemporary poet (no gravestone, just ashes), you can hear the tetrameter (4 beats) rhythm of Yeats, on whose broad shoulders stand most of the poets of our time. I couldn't have written this if I hadn't memorized his poems.

Epitaph
Below these live oak branches lie
a poet's ashes pale and dry
He loved the feel of books in hand
but saw his words
as driven sand

Still he dreams as you pass by
although you may be far from home
that if you pause to read this poem
the leaves might nod
and understand

–from *Lucky Bones*, by Peter Meinke, U. of Pittsburgh Press, 2014

EASY TO BUY, AR-15

JUNE 23, 2016

Mass Murder, Again

For poetry makes nothing happen: it survives
In the valley of its making where executives
Would never want to tamper, flows on south
From ranches of isolation and the busy griefs,
Raw towns that we believe and die in; it survives,
A way of happening, a mouth . . .

   –from "In Memory of W. B. Yeats" by W. H. Auden (1907-1973)

   Aurora, Blacksburg, Columbine, "towns that we believe and die in": easy as A B C. Charleston, Killeen, Newtown sound as musical as San Bernardino, San Ysidro, and now Orlando. Every time the blood gushes, people turn to poetry, as they should. Poetry's the emotional history of the world, and what causes more emotion than the slaughter of innocents? It has always been thus. One of our great Biblical stories is about the slaying of the male babies by Herod the Great (the *Great*!) in Bethlehem; the weeping was great, and the art that followed, such as Pieter Breughel's "Massacre of the Innocents," was also great. Statisticians have told us that more poems were written after 9/11 than at any other time in the history of America.

   I'm tired of it. We need more than poetry now. "Poetry makes nothing happen" isn't quite right, of course, as it makes us more aware, more thoughtful, and assuages our sorrow with beauty and insight. But so far, in America, it hasn't affected our suicidally stupid laws about guns. And there's a chance that we're even heading in the wrong direction.

I'm old enough to remember Senator Joe McCarthy, an ex-Marine who liked to be photographed in fighting gear with machine gun ammunition wrapped in belts around his substantial belly. The memory came back when I heard the Republican nominee speak about the Orlando tragedy at the Pulse night club. While other speakers spoke in sympathy for the dead and wounded, and their families; and some brought up specific plans (banning assault weapons, tightening the sale of weapons, etc.), Donald Trump came out blazing with a tirade against Muslims (branding them all as threats), but also with a bizarre, McCarthyesque implication that President Obama was behind the whole thing. His speech was blatantly false (pick your own example), oblivious of the LGBT victims, and focused entirely on fanning the flames of hate, fear, and suspicion on top of the smoldering racism he's been cultivating ever since he promoted the "birther" rumor that Obama was a Kenyan communist trying to destroy America.

Where are the Republicans on this speech? Many must be upset, but what about the "leaders": Speaker Paul Ryan, Majority Leader Mitch McConnell, Florida's own Senator Marco Rubio (thinking of jumping in once more)? "We still endorse him. He'll come around," they're telling us. No, he won't. We need them to confront Trump in the way that Joseph Welsh confronted McCarthy: "Have you no sense of decency, sir, at long last? Have you left no sense of decency?"

The McCarthy anti-communist saga stays fresh with me because Edward R. Murrow spoke at Hamilton College in 1954, after he had bravely exposed McCarthy on CBS News. I was just a feckless student, attracted to Murrow because he was funny, soft-spoken, chain-smoked and drank scotch—the Humphrey Bogart of journalism. But his eloquence penetrated through the fog of our youthful callowness, and his ideas planted seeds that rolled around in the dark for a while before starting to grow.

So, my dears, keep writing and reading poetry, keep the tributes coming for the victims whose future happiness, loves and losses have been wiped out; but, in addition, we need action. Think of Switzerland where, with universal military service, there's a rifle in every front closet, but not an AR-15 anywhere to be found.

Don't let your vote be suppressed. We don't have to go backwards. In November, look up and down the voting list. Vote from top to bottom. Think of the way each party, and each individual, will approach our gun control nightmare, remember Pulse and Sandy Hook and Virginia Tech and Umpqua Community College and Emanuel African American Episcopal Church; and vote.

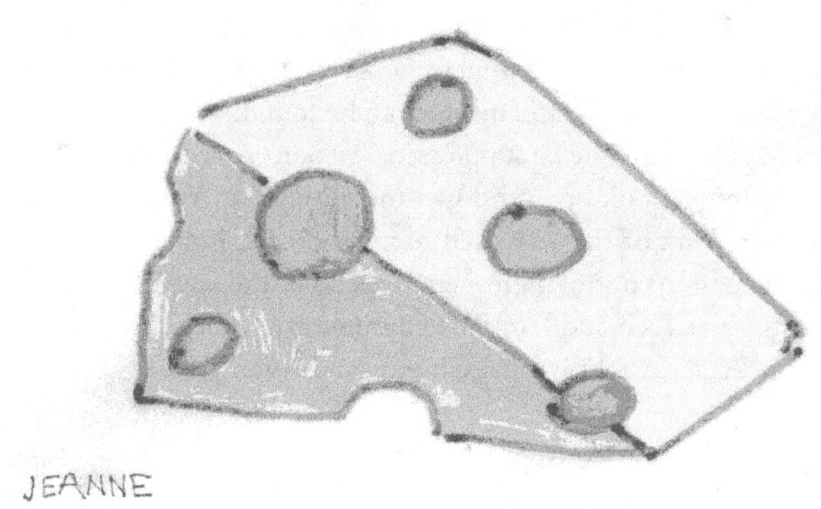

SWISS CHEESE

JULY 7, 2016

A Friend in Cheeses

"Virginity breeds mice, much like a cheese."
  –Said by Parolles in *All's Well That Ends Well*, by
  William Shakespeare

Last April, when my sister Carol asked me how I was doing, I complained I was overworked from giving so many readings because it was National Poetry Month. Unimpressed by this vision of exhausted poets around the country, she pointed out that it was also National Grilled Cheese Month. Who knew?

"Isn't that interesting?" she asked.

Actually it is. For one thing, it helps cut against the irony of all these month-long celebrations, like Human Trafficking Month (January), Black History Month (February), Women's History Month (March), etc. Shouldn't we think of these things more often, and read a poem outside of April?

It's like putting the Commandments on the calendar: In March, we'll stop swearing; in June we shall not kill; in July we won't commit adultery... Well, we're a pretty forgetful country—how *did* we get into Iraq?—and can use reminders. That's why we have these irritating National Months, and Post-it Notes.

On the other hand, it's delightful to hear about "Weight Loss Awareness Month" (January), "National Forestry Mulcher Month" (February), not to mention "National Ice Cream Month" (July). Some odd ones make us smile, like "Alopecia Awareness Month"

(September), as we have a friend with that condition—bodily hair loss—who enjoys getting some publicity about his obscure disease.

Talking with Carol helped me realize that, despite growing up in Brooklyn on a diet of Kraft pre-cut orange-colored cheese sandwiches on soft white Wonder Bread, real cheese has played a frequent part in our gustatory and imaginative lives. In the Army, stationed in Germany in 1956, a friend and I took a long weekend furlough to Paris, which we had experienced only in novels and dreams. An image that pops up, from early in our visit, is of us sitting on the steps of Montmartre with a baguette, a bottle of cheap red wine, and a very smelly hunk of Camembert cheese we bought randomly at an exotic and crowded "*Crèmerie.*" It tasted strange and strong, and we wondered, do we hold our noses, do we eat this rind? This (or the wine) made us laugh, and as we passed the bottle and washed the gummy cheese and chewy bread down, we couldn't have been happier sitting at the bar in The Four Seasons.

Fifteen years later, the Meinke family went to Neuchâtel, Switzerland, for a year. Right away, we went to the neighborhood tavern, Le Café du Pont, and ordered the *specialité* of the city, cheese fondue, which we'd never tasted. With it, I ordered beer for us, and milk for the children. The waiter exploded with indignation. "*Mais non, monsieur, pas de la bière, pas du lait*! *Seul le vin blanc ou de l'eau.!* Cheese fondue is now one of Jeanne's specialties, and I always recite to our guests: "No beer! No milk! Only white wine or water!" (And once, when a guest observed that fondue must be a lot of work, Jeanne said, It's not so bad, pointing out that I cut the bread and grate the cheese. At which, our late dear friend Ken Keeton raised his hand and solemnly pronounced, "Ah yes, Peter the Grater!"). This, too, alas, has stayed in the family.

One other cheese ritual takes us to England. Every two weeks we drive to Mazzaro's to pick up the items for our biweekly "Ploughman's Lunch": a couple of apples or pears, a chutney with kick, maybe a pickle or two, some fresh crusty bread, and a wedge of Stilton Cheese. We already have some Smithwick's Irish Ale in the refrigerator.

Once home, we'll spread these out on our wooden kitchen countertop. I'll pop the Smithwick's, we'll sit down, click our glasses, and immediately fly 4000 miles: Hello Dove Pub, hi Patricia, hey Damien—great to be in London again! What's up?

> *What a friend we have in cheeses,*
> *Mozzarella, Cheddar, Swiss!*
> *Bleu and Limberger's sweet breezes*
> *Lingering like a lover's kiss …*
>
> –from a traditional parody @ The Mudcat Café.org

FBI DIRECTOR JAMES COMEY

JULY 21, 2016

Greatness

I am the poet of the slaves
and of the masters of slaves.
I am the poet of the body
and poet of the soul.

Walt Whitman said "To have great poets, there must be great audiences." In his case, though the audience for poetry was small, it had real influence; and it took very little time for Whitman to be recognized as a major poet. (Poetry's audience today is larger, but spread thinner, and has even less influence.)

Still, in poetry, the opposite of every rule can also be true, as in life—"Look before you leap," but "He who hesitates is lost." (Even in science, a light can be a particle and a wave at the same time.) F. Scott Fitzgerald observed that the "test of a first-rate intelligence is the ability to hold two opposing ideas in mind at the same time and still retain the ability to function." Whew!

W. H. Auden wrote, about W. B. Yeats, "Mad Ireland hurt you into poetry"; and it's probable that Whitman's nursing wounded and dying soldiers during the Civil War had a stronger influence on his poetry than his "great audience." It's telling, with Attorney General Loretta Lynch in the news, that Whitman, about to fall into debt, was kept afloat by Lincoln's Attorney General, James Speed, who appointed him clerk in Speed's office, a job Whitman held until his final illness. Poets' lives matter!

Fitzgerald's quote is a perfect description of President Obama's balancing act, as he reacts to our country's latest catastrophes, and, in fact, of how he's had to operate from the beginning as our first black president, facing the most antagonistic congress in history.

I'm writing this just as the Republican convention's beginning, so who knows what will happen there? But the very *idea* of "greatness" today is severely weakened. Donald Trump uses "great" so much that the word tastes like a poisoned lollipop: "I'll build a great, great wall"; "I've always had a great relationship with blacks"; "You have to be wealthy in order to be great," etc. At least the Republicans are recognizing that Trump is *their* Frankenstein: they created him, and they own him, so the convention should be fascinating as a snake pit. Whatever else Trump may be, he's the opposite of a calming, unifying influence. Even sending in his gorgeous wife Melania has backfired, sabotaged by Trump's plagiarizing speech writers.

The Republicans treatment of FBI Director James Comey earlier this month showed that they can't even recognize common decency, much less greatness. Comey, originally appointed by President Bush, is an old-style Republican—conservative, patriotic, direct—and bent over backward to give the committee some ammunition on Clinton while clearly explaining why none of it was criminal or prosecutable. Just as they did when questioning Clinton about Benghazi and Lynch about the emails, the congressmen were bullying, petty, and partisan.

This is why their base has turned to Trump. The country yearns for legislation on jobs, climate change, infrastructure, immigration, and equal rights, but the Republicans spent the last seven years wasting millions of taxpayers' dollars and uncountable hours—almost their entire effort—on multiple committees trying to overthrow Obamacare (despite the Supreme Court's decision); trying to destroy Clinton over Benghazi (despite every one coming up empty); and trying to convict her of email treachery (with zero success). Now, with Comey's and the FBI's hardly friendly but fair and legal exoneration of Clinton, they're ready to start again! Far from greatness, it's the old definition of insanity. They pay no attention to the bipartisan Politifact, which shows Clinton as the most truthful speaker on actual policies, and Trump as (by far) the least.

As President Obama nears the end of his reign, his attempts at bridging the racial and social divides in our country are being more appreciated. "Great" or not, like Whitman and Martin Luther King, Obama's moderate voice and gentle eloquence have prodded us to become better people, and better citizens.

I go with the slaves
equally with the masters
that both will understand me alike.

–both quotes from "Leaves of Grass" by Walt Whitman (1819-1892)

MORTARBOARD

AUGUST 11, 2016

Education

It's June: the universities
to prove the sun can shine
are hanging their late bloomers
on the academic line . . .

The angry masses that the Republicans and Democrats have raked up in this hellish election are basically different crowds. The kids who felt the Bern are the about-to-be educated children of the middle class, sliding into college debt and reading Karl Marx's *Das Kapital* about the rich eating the poor. The jobs they're studying for are either taken or poorly paid, while CEO's are knocking down bonuses fit for a king, or even a football coach. Lacking their parents' and grandparents' instinctive revulsion to European Socialism, they flocked to Bernie, not least because what he says is—to quote PolitiFact—"Mostly True." Of course, he didn't explain how much it will cost, or the damage they might cause if they don't join forces with Hillary Clinton. See Ralph Nader, 2000.

Those who twitter with Trump, on the other hand, have found they've been simply crowded out of the boat; they haven't been taught to swim in turbulent water, and people who don't look like them are stroking smoothly by, grabbing the life preservers. Their situation seems like sink or swim: it's not fair.

Life isn't fair, never has been. America, however, has slipped backward, spending its vast wealth carelessly and heartlessly. But we have a chance to be fair-ish again: With decent education, democracy can work. The Bernie supporters will have to support Clinton, who'll help them get jobs, and pay for their college bills. The Trump supporters need work, too—but first, most of them need education, and help in getting back to school. No matter who wins, those manufacturing jobs aren't coming back.

Within our own extended family, there's general agreement about open and fair immigration, and free and fair education. Multiple countries have joined our family tree in just two generations—Chinese, Japanese, Filipino, Pakistani, and others—and their stories bring credit to America. We're a middle class family with blue-collar beginnings (our grandparents sailed from Europe in the 19th century) that bet big on education; it seems obvious that the mix of sensible immigration and easy access to good schools is the best path ahead.

We have two brilliant daughters-in-law, Aya Aoki from Tokyo, and Wei Chu from Taipei. Wei's story is typical. Born in Taiwan, the 3rd of 4 children, she was just a child when her father died. When she was 17, the family followed relatives and moved to New York. The children had studied English, but studying English in Taiwan and speaking it when you're thrown into a big American city are very different things. Nevertheless, although her SAT English scores were "modest," she scored a perfect 800 on the math section. "Education was everything to us," she told us, and this dedication was evident to savvy college admissions counselors, who could see that her English would come along—she understood those math questions!—and offered her financial aid to attend their schools.

For this, we feel proud of America. It's the way our system should work. An immigrant arrives, works and studies hard, and is rewarded; which in turn makes America stronger. She wound up going to Johns Hopkins, through its college and med school; she's now Dr. Wei Chu, married into the infamous Meinke clan.

"Education was everything to us" needs to catch on with Americans. The next president has to tackle our programs from pre-school to grad school. (So far, Clinton has a plan; Trump's said zero.) We'll have to bite the tax bullet, recognizing that our education, not our military, is primarily what will keep America great. And although I have some fun with this poem about my own studies, our motto should be No Drones in School.

> *I took our daughter Gretchen out*
>   *and our son whatsisname*
> *I lost them in the stacks somehow*
>   *Home's never been the same*
>
> *Now I'm alone but free at last*
>   *to wander in the meadows*
> *the world's leading authority*
>   *on Thomas Lovell Beddoes*

    –both quotes from "On Completing My PhD" by Peter Meinke, from *Lucky Bones*, U. of Pittsburgh Press, 2014

PETER'S DESK WITH POST-IT NOTES

AUGUST 18, 2016

Post Master

Watch steps.

—Post-it Note stuck on upstairs staircase in the Meinke household

I bet you didn't know that tomorrow (August 19th) is Arthur Fry's birthday. *Arthur Fry?* you ask. Well, he's only the guy who invented those little yellow squares we all use: Post-it Notes.

How did we ever manage without Post-it Notes? The ubiquitous stickers have crept up on me, but I scarcely acknowledged them until Jeanne confronted me with this photo of my desk. Jeanne has an artist's eye, and notices things like that. She uses them, too but lines them up neatly on our kitchen counter (shopping lists), on our calendar (dates to remember), and her work table (drawing ideas).

I myself use them randomly and they pile up around my desk like autumn leaves in Vermont.

Typical of many Eureka moments, the idea for these famous stickems came about like a gift from heaven; and this one actually arrived in church. In 1973 Fry was a research scientist at Minnesota Mining & Manufacturing, and went to a seminar given by another 3M scientist, Spencer Silver. Silver had been working on a strong adhesive that could be used in building planes, when he accidentally developed a weak one, called Acrylate Copolymer Microspheres (wonderful name!) that peeled off without leaving sticky marks, and could be reused. But nobody had figured out a way to use it.

Fry sang in his church choir at nights, and used pieces of paper to mark the pages. One Sunday, shortly after the seminar, Fry picked up his hymnbook and some of his makeshift bookmarks fell out, as they often did. As with Saul on the road to Damascus, the scales fell from Fry's eyes, and he saw clearly: Silver's adhesive would make a better bookmark.

The next day he acquired some samples of the adhesive, and applied it to one edge of the page. He fiddled around with it for some weeks, eventually using yellow squares (another accident: the lab next door had a big pile of yellow paper left over from something else—and this worked, obviously, much better than white on white). It didn't take long for the yellow Post-it note to be born. There's a charming photo online of Mr. Fry beaming, with a Post-it note fixed on his balding head.

The use of these notes grew quickly and colorfully; and are still ubiquitous despite the proliferation of iphones, which carry unlimited information in our pockets. Studio 620 even put on a play about a couple addicted to Post-it Notes, concluding with the actors covered head to foot with pieces of paper, looking like old scarecrows, or maybe Puritan minister Jonathan Edwards, who while making calls on horse-back would pin notes for his sermons and poems on his clothes, organizing them when he fluttered into town.

Fry's little notes arrived in time for an aging America, where close to 50 million citizens are over 65, as far as they can remember, anyway. It's certain my use of these yellow markers has increased like, and with, the gray hairs on my head. We've lived in our two-story house for almost 50 years, and many friends worry about our wooden staircase leading down to tile floors (my mother once climbed up them on her hands and knees). "You're going to forget your age, run down the stairs, and break a hip," is the warning. On the other hand, now that we, and especially me, with my "office" on the second floor, have become more forgetful, going up and down the staircase is my main exercise. So, if I don't actually tumble down the steps and through

the window onto our brick patio, it's good for me. I keep meaning to stick a Post-It note at the top saying "Think before you step." ...
I think I'll stick it on right now.

So Happy Birthday Arthur Fry
Some make buildings   some build boats
some design planes that fly
and you invented Post-it Notes
You meant it helpfully that day
to organize us more or less ...

(I had something else to say
but lost the sticker in this mess)

ENOUGH ALREADY!

SEPTEMBER 1, 2016

Evolutionary Politics

... Only the human brain
dreaming the freedom of gulls & robins
can rattle the chemical chain
that binds the flow of our bones ...

Every day in my email, a friend sends me a gorgeous nature photograph, with a quote from The Urantia Book (a kind of New Age Bible and Spiritual Encyclopedia). This morning's quote was "Be not discouraged—Evolution is still in progress," along with a photo of a Bali Hai-like lagoon with small mountain islands diminishing in the blue distance. This was welcome advice.

I *was* feeling discouraged, because I'd thought that America was beyond producing *leaders* like Donald Trump. I knew we produced "Trumps"—hey, we've all met a few—but didn't believe they could wind up being more than a Dragon in the Ku Klux Klan, like David Duke cheerleading a feckless Den of Southern sheetlovers. In 2008, when the Republicans picked Sarah Palin, I figured Barack Obama would win, despite John McCain's likability and Obama's blackness. Politically speaking, Palin was a step back on the evolutionary ladder.

The Donald would take us *three* steps back.

Disappointingly, the coalition of Cro-Magnons who loved Palin has grown, fueled by economic and psychological depression and the Republicans' united refusal to welcome, or even respect, their twice-elected president. Covert racial prejudice was given a cover as "honest" rebuttals of political correctness. "You lie," shouted Joe Wilson, after President Obama made a clearly truthful statement about the Immigration Bill under discussion. South Carolina has re-elected him ever since.

Donald Trump started building his presidential qualifications by forging the "birther" movement, again a ridiculous idea—and a straight intentional lie—easily disproved, but swallowed by millions, like the huge wall that Mexico will pay for. These Trump followers don't exactly believe this nonsense, but are following their *deeper* "truth": A black man has no business being President. "Making America great again" won't involve an America led by a black man, or a woman of any color.

Even Bernie Sanders, whom we hoped would lead us forward toward better control of banks and single payer health insurance, acted as if he had forgotten how to count. Long after the race was over (back in April when Clinton swept through New York, Pennsylvania, Maryland and Connecticut), he kept fanning the flames by insisting to his young followers that "We're going to win!" He could have stayed in the "race" attacking Trump, but instead he fanned false hope in his millions of young math-deprived fans who now think the system's rigged. It's not a great system, but it wasn't "rigged" against Bernie, who was simply outvoted. (Of course the leaked NDC emails showed a pro-Clinton bias—they've been working for her for years, while Bernie wasn't even a Democrat.) Bernie now should try to convince his fans—with conviction—that Hillary's not "the lesser of two evils." In his concession speech, on stage with Clinton, he talked so long about himself before conceding, we were hoping she'd kick him in the shins to hurry him along.

"Crooked Hillary," "Pocahontas," "Little Marco," "Low Energy Jeb" aren't political ideas; they're playground bullying, and the media should send Trump to the principal's office. Many Republicans seem ready to do this.

Evolution always has its victims (dinosaurs, model T's, land phones), and the human genus is still developing. Starved serfs, burned martyrs, enslaved blacks, degraded gays, and women demeaned for centuries: civilization's slowly edging up, with the help of democratic (small and big "d") politics. Evolution's real (and real slow), and where it's headed is seldom clear: With Trump and his followers flouting their and our primitive instincts, we need to prevent them from nudging it in the wrong direction.

> *. . . while visions sweep like birds*
> *trapped in a skull-like cave*
> *wingtips brushing the walls*
> *the night going mad with their cries*
> *till a few of the strongest & luckiest*
> *skip like stones from our eyes . . .*

> –both quotes from "The Chemical Chain" by Peter Meinke, in *The Contracted World: New & More Selected Poems* (U. of Pittsburgh Press, 2006)

ONION SOUP FOR EDWARD FIELD

SEPTEMBER 15, 2016

Poet Edward Field

The day Edward Field came to dinner
I polished the hell out of the kitchen table
and wore my best casual clothes but no tie . . .

Now kids I said Dammit this guy's a poet
and sensitive and a bachelor and I don't want
you to scream or jump on his stomach . . .

When asked by youngsters who seem genuinely interested in "growing up" to be a poet, I mostly give them the same boring answers: Hang in there, just keep writing; also read a lot, especially poetry.

Good advice, but I'm not sure it's always true. I've met decent poets (admittedly rare) who haven't read much. And I've known a few who don't write steadily, but more or less when the mood strikes them.

I've thought of telling them they shouldn't "grow up" at all, as poetry's occasionally labeled an adolescent activity, written by maladjusted individuals whose mixture of wonder and rebellion is basically childlike. I still tend to look at Florida's clouds, and go "Woof!" I usually don't tell them that.

But lately I've been telling students about meeting Edward Field, the first "real" poet I got to know well. Around 1973, Florida Presbyterian College found some extra money to bring in a visiting writer. President Billy Wireman, who, through his friendship with Jack Eckerd, had just saved "financially struggling FPC" (as the *St. Pete Times* referred us), called me into his office. The college was changing its name from Florida Presbyterian to Eckerd, and Billy's ambition was to make our small religion-based school into a nationally competitive liberal arts college.

"Find me a reputable and not too expensive poet," Billy said. This would be good advertising for our new undergraduate degree in Creative Writing. I'd just bought Field's *Stand Up, Friend, With Me*, winner of the prestigious Lamont Poetry Award, and Field had also written the narration for Walt Disney's documentary film, *To Be Alive*, which won an Academy Award. How reputable can you get! Billy told me to call him right away, before the money was grabbed by another department.

The next morning I found Field's number and dialed it, but I was nervous. The previous evening I'd read his book, and loved it. But the poems showed clearly that I'd be offering a teaching job in St. Petersburg—where in those days "people came to die"—at a school still often called Florida Presbyterian, to a poet who was a gay Jewish bohemian who lived in Greenwich Village: probably not the best fit! I was hoping no one would answer: he was going to laugh at me. But after the fourth ring, a mellow voice said, "Good morning."

"Hello, Mr. Field," I stuttered, and plunged on. "My name's Peter Meinke and I'm calling to offer you a semester's teaching appointment at Eckerd College, better known as Florida Presbyterian, in St. Petersburg . . ." I stopped, not quite sure I should bother finishing the sentence.

After a short pause, Edward Field, who had never heard of either me or the school, said, "Oh Peter, "you're not going to believe this, but just this very morning I took a vow to say yes to everything!"

Well, Edward came to our college, and the students loved him, as did we; he's now "Greenwich Village's oldest Bohemian," as *The New Yorker* recently called him, and still writing and traveling around the world with his partner, Neil Derrick.

Poetry pries open the shut windows of the world, so it can enter into our homes. Saying yes to the world doesn't always mean agreeing with it, but welcoming it with affection and generosity. I recognize that it's not possible to say yes on every occasion, but for a poet it's a pretty good first principle.

> *Waiting for him to arrive I sat on my hands for half an hour*
> *warming them up for the handshake*
> *Finally the doorbell rang*
> *I opened the door and there he was!*
>
> *Hello I said I hope you like onion soup*
>
> –both quotes from "The Day Edward Field Came to Dinner" in *Trying to Surprise God* by Peter Meinke (U. of Pittsburgh Press, 1981)

BRASSERIE DU PONT

SEPTEMBER 29, 2016

Suicide

all my plans for suicide are ridiculous
I can never remember the heart's location
too cheap to crash the car
too queasy to slash a wrist
once jumped off a bridge
almost scared myself to death
then spent two foggy weeks
waiting for new glasses

of course I really want to live
continuing my lifelong search
for the world's greatest unknown cheap restaurant
and a poem full of ordinary words
about simple things
in the inconsolable rhythms of the heart

–"The Heart's Location," from *The Night Train & the Golden Bird*, by Peter Meinke (U. of Pittsburgh Press, 1977)

My first book of poetry began with a poem, "The Night Train," about suicides committed on trains. It's a skinny book, and though (as you know) I'm a pleasantly cheerful person, it included a heavy amount of dark poems. When asked about this, I generally answer, "Because I wrote most of them after midnight."

Back then, Jeanne and I had four small children. She was dealing with them through long Minnesota winters (1961-66); our president, John F. Kennedy, was assassinated; the Vietnam War was escalating;

and I was teaching Freshman English full time and studying for my Ph. D. When we think we're busy these days, and a bit politically discouraged, we sometimes look back on those years and shake our heads. Oddly enough, we were very happy.

Sitting there writing (and smoking and sipping Jim Beam—this was before Healthy Habits sprouted) in the dark and quiet house, I knew I was surrounded by a loving, and often hilarious, family. I wasn't at all suicidal, but the subject would come up in my writing. Who doesn't think about it somewhere along the line?

Of course I was reading John Keats *("for many a time / I have been half in love with easeful Death")*, Robert Frost (*"With a lantern that wouldn't burn / In too frail a buggy we drove / Behind too heavy a horse / Through a pitch-dark limitless grove,"* and other darkling poets; but the subject came up because I was also attracted to the writing of Albert Camus, the Nobel Prize-winning French writer who'd been killed in 1960 in a car accident.

Camus theorized that the only serious philosophical question is that of suicide. His view of life was summed up by the myth of Sisyphus, who pushed his boulder up a mountain only to have it roll back when he reached the top (the cheerier American version has Charlie Brown endlessly setting up his football, which Lucy then snatches away). In the end, Camus seemed to repudiate suicide by simply accepting the absurdity of life. Well, why not? This was fascinating stuff to a struggling young writer.

These ideas came rolling back to me like a Sisyphean boulder while reading recent reports of great increases in American suicides, first among the military (alarming but understandable); then of white males (headline: White, Middle-age Suicide in America Skyrockets); and finally, the rise of America's mortality rate in general, pushed by our own Four Horsemen of the Apocalypse—Depression, Drugs, Alzheimer's, and Suicide.

Depression is the mother of despair, and for a country as rich as ours, it's a sin that we haven't fought it harder. Donald Trump has fattened on it. For the bulk of these depressed persons, it isn't money or race, exactly, but a lack of hope and progress, coupled with the natural desire to be doing something useful. (This is the retirement home problem: people mulling about, not uncomfortable, but directionless.)

Even at our poorest, Jeanne and I felt we were going somewhere, headed in the "right" direction, though we had no idea what that was. And, while the search never ends, we did find at least one of the world's "great unknown cheap restaurants," a workers' café in Neuchâtel, Switzerland, serving the laborers from the city and the Suchard Factory, plus its neighbors like us. A five-minute walk from our house on Quai Suchard, an affordable hour there with thoughtful waiters, terrific food, a liberal use of garlic and wine; and all felt right with our expanding world.

BROKEN GLASSES

OCTOBER 13 2016

Loose Notes

Why are the stamps adorned
with kings and presidents?
That we may lick their hinder parts
and thump their heads.

–from "Power to the People" by Howard Nemerov (1920-1991)

When I started doing these *Note*books, that's what I had in mind: short notes about various subjects like art, family, and politics, in small bites; though they soon developed into a loose essay format. As the torture of this endless election winds to its painful close, here's a throwback to semi-related notes that I haven't been able to fit in the essays. After all, I only have 700 words to do these things.

• I've been in hundreds of locker rooms, and I'm not surprised to see that just as Donald Trump has lowered the bar for political discourse throughout this long distasteful year, he's even succeeded lowering the bar for "locker-room talk" as well. His vocabulary may be similar, but his crass and selfish appetite is the worst I've ever heard, even in locker rooms.

• In America, it's a crime to shout "fire" in a crowded hall, but the Donald regularly shouts "Obama and Hillary are the founders of ISIS!" and "Lock her up!" to throngs of armed and undereducated hotheads. If Clinton's elected, he hints, "Nothing you can do, folks—although the 2nd Amendment people, maybe there is . . ."

• People compare Trump to Joe McCarthy, Putin, even Mussolini, but his constant disparagement of the media and the educated ("I love uneducated people") reminds me of Pol Pot, the murderous leader of Cambodia's Khmer Rouge, who hated not just "intellectuals," but anyone who wore glasses, so hordes of Cambodians broke their glasses and stumbled around to avoid getting purged.

• Ignorance of the uneducated is natural—*Nobody taught them nothin'*—but the ignorance of the rich is chosen. The poor don't believe in Global Warming because they see snow in the winter; the rich don't believe in it (see Rubio, Scott, Trump, *et al.*) because they're not "scientists," *i.e.*, their money comes from billionaires who depend on Big Oil.

• The difference between the parties is that the Republicans nominated Trump while the Democrats rejected Sanders. Psychologically, the GOP went with its gut, while the Dems stuck with its head. This is a reversal of the intellectual tradition of the Right. We grew up watching William Buckley's "Firing Line," where serious ideas got intelligently, and often wittily, debated.

• Recently I pulled out Edgar Allan Poe's book of poems, the one I loved when I first started reading by flashlight in my little room in Brooklyn. But the poems seemed heavily out-of-date—*Lo, Death has reared himself a throne*—with faults sticking out of his lines like a pot belly on an old flame. But Emily Dickinson sounds contemporary.

• Trump, like Poe (and unlike Dickinson) has no sense of humor. He often says he's "joking," but that's just another straight lie: he's simply taking back some coarse insult made the previous day. Buffoonery's gross: the humor of heroes is quiet (John Kennedy and Obama, for example; or Humphrey Bogart in "Casablanca" or even that Republican Clint Eastwood in "Dirty Harry"). Trump saying that New York Times columnist Gail Collins has "the face of a dog" isn't funny.

• Today's troubles began 400 years ago when Copernicus and Galileo proved that the earth moved around the sun, rather than vice versa. Since then it's been believers against unbelievers, patriarchy against feminism, the Bible against *The Double Helix*. But the pace and heat of this debate have been picking up: the Good Old Days (GOD?) against LGBTQ.

• Muslims are our friends, allies, and relatives. Islamic terrorists are just the mad dogs of Islam that need to be quarantined or exterminated the way the law handled Timothy McVeigh and the Tsarnaev brothers.

• Watching Trump pick on people more or less at random, I was reminded of Tom Buchanan in F. Scott Fitzgerald's *The Great Gatsby*. Buchanan—a prejudiced bully who inherited his money—with his wife Daisy "smashed up things and creatures and then retreated back into their money or their vast carelessness, or whatever it was that kept them together and let other people clean up the mess they made." Literature prepares us for what might happen.

> *Of the Great World he knew not much,*
> *But his Muse let little in language escape her.*
> *Friends sigh and say of him, poor wretch,*
> *He was a good writer, on paper.*
>
> –from "Epitaph" by Howard Nemerov

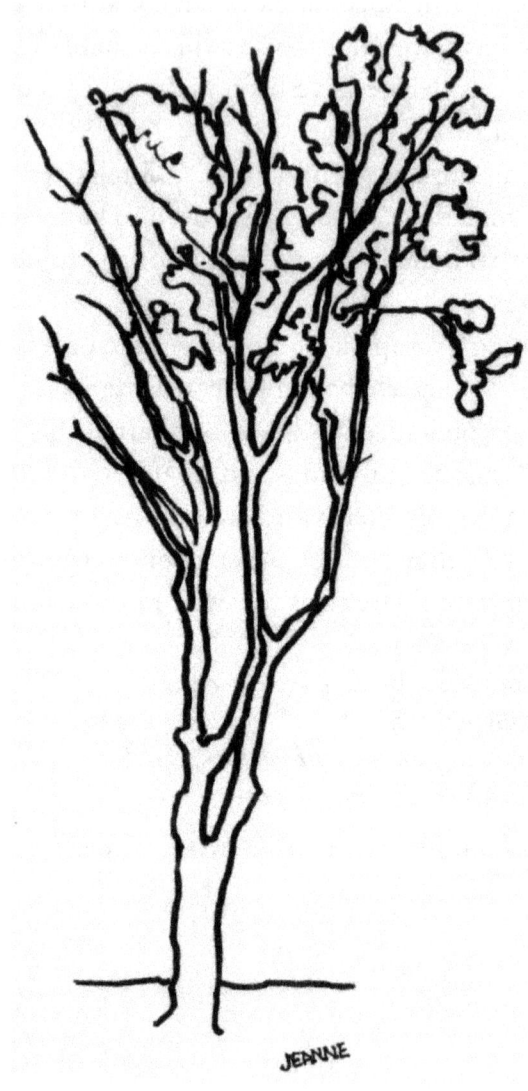

OLD TREE

OCTOBER 27, 2016

Old Age

That time of year thou mayst in me behold
When yellow leaves, or none, or few do hang
Upon those boughs which shake against the cold,
Bare ruined choirs where late the sweet birds sang.

When I was a young man the Shakespeare poem I memorized as I lay awake at night was "Sonnet 18," which begins, "Shall I compare thee to a summer's day?" You never could tell when that might come in handy. But now in my dozing dotage I find myself murmuring "Sonnet 73" (above and below), a dark meditation on the sunset years, which seems well aimed at Floridians who gather on the Hurricane's deck to watch the sun go down over Tampa Bay. Amazingly (everything about Shakespeare's amazing), he probably wrote "#73" in his early 30's (he was only 52 when he died). How did he know so much about old age when he was basically just a kid? It's the same sort of genius-dust that Stephen Crane sniffed while writing *The Red Badge of Courage* without ever having fought in a war.

Human beings, blessed and cursed with imagination, have always longed for immortality. We'll do almost anything to live a little longer. The most honest among us are those like Woody Allen, who observed that "I don't want to achieve immortality through my works—I want to achieve it by not dying." A few thousand rich Americans are betting on cryopreservation (freezing after death), with the hope that medical science will figure out how to revive them in the future.

This is as unlikely as America voting for Trump to be president, and almost as scary.

We often hear that "60 is the new 40" and, recently, "70 is the new 50." We don't hear much about the 80's, the group we travel with, twirling canes and adjusting hearing aids (a not infrequent squeal at poetry readings). My own experience tells me that 80 is the new 79.

In any case, when we look at the ads on TV or in magazines, the models all seem to be 19 or younger, ignoring the 40's and 50's, especially the new ones. So America's offering us a paradoxical deal: As we age we're looking younger than we used to, but not young enough to be appealing to customers. Looks aren't everything: I said to our doctor, who complimented us when we entered his office, "We look better than we feel."

Lately, I've had to go to a chiropractor who works in a large rectangular brick building with narrow hallways and many doors for offices and treatment; in short, for the elderly, a maze. Even after several visits, I still go the wrong way to get to the exit, like a retarded mouse in a scientific study. Nurses emerge and gently prod me around. Since I hadn't fallen or bumped anything hard, I asked my doctor how I had injured my hip; he looked at me kindly and said, "Bad luck."

The undeniable difficulties of old age are speedily becoming much more common: life expectancy when we were born was less than 60; today it's over 80. But nowadays the difficulties seem worse, the physical and mental deterioration doubled like compound interest by what's happening to America. Our political system's suffering from arteriosclerosis and osteoporosis at once. All of us, Democrats and Republicans alike, loved, worked for, marched for, and believed in our country. These days, large numbers of both sides look around with apprehension, while loneliness is spreading like the measles.

And yet, I think poetry (or whichever art works for you) can help. Its thrust is acceptance, connection, vulnerability. *Whose woods these are I think I know.* I don't *know* I know; I just think so. Dictators and demagogues, who always know everything, are always against poetry. *Lock 'em up!*

Poets, especially old poets, are against the death penalty.

> *In me thou see'st the glowing of such fire*
> *That on the ashes of his youth doth lie*
> *As the death-bed whereon it must expire,*
> *Consumed with that which it was nourished by . . .*
>
> –both quotes from *Sonnet 73* by William Shakespeare (1564-1616)

HILLARY CLINTON AND TIM KAINE

NOVEMBER 10, 2016

Trump Wins!

Mine—by the Right of the White Election!
Mine—by the Royal Seal!
Mine—by the sign of the Scarlet prison—
Bars—cannot conceal!

I like to think that Hillary Rodham, when she was a serious young student, read Emily Dickinson's poem. (Emily *who*? says the Donald, scratching his belly). In it, the quiet and overlooked (in her lifetime) Dickinson is shouting in almost Trumpian tones "Hey, I did it! Ignore me *now*!" Great writers, even mousy ones, often have total confidence in their poems. These lines are similar, though more exultant, to Shakespeare's conclusion of his "Sonnet 18": "So long as men can breathe, or eyes can see, / So long lives this, and this gives life to thee." In Dickinson's poem, though, there's a more contemporary note, a defiant feminist recklessness, a passionate in-your-face exhilaration.

Exhilaration? Despite the subtle smuggling of Hillary's name into the word, there's no "exhilaration" here after this soul-crushing defeat. Not even relief that it's over: America has chosen a man completely estranged from our former ideals of statesmanship (not to mention common decency). Whatever you think of President Obama's policies, one glance at him and his family conveys intelligence, class, and grace. The realization that the boorish coarseness of Donald Trump is replacing him is horrific.

Hillary Clinton and Tim Caine seemed steady and prepared to follow in Obama's footsteps for the difficult work ahead. With some help from Congress, we might actually have prospered! (Compared to the rest of the world, we're already doing well.) Of course, they would have watched Clinton's emails like a hawk, maybe appointing several permanent Republican committees to read each one as it headed out.

This election was a victory for a party that did nothing for eight years besides attack Obama and Clinton, wasting taxpayers' money on phony targets, while setting problems like climate change, education, and gun laws back at least a generation. And now, encouraged by FBI Director James Comey's unprecedented double entry into this election with his late partisan bombshell—which may well have turned the election—the GOP has lowered the bar for allowable political behavior for decades to come. All we have left is Saturday Night Live.

Post-election, we'll have a largely unhappy citizenry who, despite great strides since the 2008 depression, are angry at the obvious inequalities in our system. Of course, they're mad at the wrong people. Every respectable study has shown that immigration is good for America, and lifts our standard of living. We can feel relieved that, while England's anger at the *other* has resulted in Brexit and a split with Europe (the cost of which is rising by the day), ours has at least a chance of being smoothed out by our inability to pass anything. We shall see.

Clinton would have been fine. A popular Senator, she worked well across the aisles. As a bonus, she would have been unlikely to dally with a page boy, knowing first-hand how such indiscretions work out in the White House (she learned about the "Scarlet prison" from Bill; Dickinson just imagined it, maybe thinking of Hester Prynne in *The Scarlet Letter*). Given half a chance, Clinton would have been a fine president, joining other leaders like Chancellor Angela Merkel (Germany), Prime Minister Theresa May (England), State Counselor Aung Sun Suu Kyi (Myanmar), President Tsai Ing-wen (Taiwan) and many others. I hope Trump can behave himself while dealing with these dignified leaders. Lord knows what they're thinking right now!

So back to Dickinson's wonderful poem. During this long, hard election year, I liked to imagine those two strong women, Emily and Hillary, holding hands on the steps of some celestial White House, our first great visionary poet with the first woman president of the United States, hands uplifted before the unknown future and the hopeful and hungry crowd.

The poem has a sadder ring now. This vision's been set far back—and a question posed: Is misogyny stronger than racism?

Mine—here—in Vision—and in Veto!
Mine—by the Grave's Repeal—
Titled—Confirmed—
Delirious Charter!
Mine—long as Ages steal!

   –poem #411 by Emily Dickinson (1830-1886)

BOB DYLAN

NOVEMBER 24, 2016

Changes

And new philosophy cast all in doubt,
The element of fire is quite put out;
The sun is lost, and th'earth, and no man's wit
Can well direct him where to look for it

  –from "An Anatomy of the World" by John Donne (1517-1631)

New York Times journalist David Brooks has often meditated on our country's moral purpose, usually without mentioning the tendency of Republican legislation to favor the rich and whack the poor. But it's a fine subject, good for all of us to think about around Thanksgiving, in between listening to Oprah and Dr. Phil.

Brooks' major point is that poetry, philosophy and religion no longer persuade or affect large numbers of people. Polls show that Christianity's losing ground to non-believers. The number seven has always been significant in Christianity (7 deadly sins, 7 parables, 7th day, 7-wick'd candelabra), and the Pew Research Center claims that in the last seven years Christianity has significantly declined: the number of "nones"—the religiously unaffiliated—has risen to be a "major force" in our society. They had a significant, though losing, role in our presidential election, lining up against the church-going Tea Party members guided by Senator Ted Cruz, a Southern Baptist. (Cruz's father leads a church in Dallas, directing a multi-country religious enterprise called the "Purifying Fire Ministries." Chubby Americans like the sound of it: burn that weight off).

But these older organizational "truths" are having trouble standing up to the test of time, and as communication become progressively faster and wider—books, radio, television, internet—we've entered a time when Donne's "all" (above) really *is* cast in doubt. Christmas is a-coming, but "holy day" has become "holiday," and seems to begin in October; bells began to jingle before the election. The very phrase, "Merry Christmas," has become political, fighting off the more generic "Happy Holidays," like Moses wrestling Santa Claus.

Poets like Donne have seen this coming for a long time. The "new philosophy" has always been with us, but until recently the doubters were in a minority. This is because our imperfect population has expanded slowly, but is picking up speed and imperfections like compound interest. When one's immersed in imperfections, they're hard to see: that's the air we breathe. Of course the world is flat: just look around. Of course global warming's a hoax: look at that snow coming down! Of course men should lead our families and governments: they're bigger and stronger! But, as our just-appointed Nobel Laureate in Literature has sung, "The times they are a-changin'."

Bob Dylan's appointment is another sign in this whirling firmament: even our idea of what makes writing "literature" is changing. When I heard the news I wasn't exactly upset (I'm a patriotic American, after all), but I did think, "Huh?" If I had been forced to nominate someone in the singing poetry category, I'd have gone for Canada's Leonard Cohen, as the more surprising and mysterious writer (now, alas, ineligible, having died on November 7th). But I'm an octogenarian, and literature to me means books; and poetry means words, standing proudly naked on a page.

Still, the more I scratched my head, the more uncertain I became. Were the songs in Shakespeare's plays not literature? *Tu-whit, tu-who': a merry note / While greasy Joan doth keel the pot.* How about Robert Burns and other lyrical poets: *Should auld acquaintance be for-*

got? I remembered that in the 60s and 70s, no writer was more influential on my students than Dylan (I'm afraid I sometimes chided them for that, to no avail). But like everyone else, I loved his songs.

I finally decided that poetry is alive, and live things grow and throw out branches. The tree of poetry is tall and has many limbs, high and low. And that harmonica player sure spotted climate change early on.

Welcome to Literature, Bob Dylan!

> *Come gather 'round people*
> *Wherever you roam*
> *And admit that the waters*
> *Around you have grown*
> *And accept it that soon*
> *You'll be drenched to the bone*
> *For the times they are a'changin'."*
>
> –lyrics from "The Times They Are A-Changin'." by Bob Dylan (1964)

FLOWERS

DECEMBER 8, 2016

Pulse: the Brillantina Project

> ... *The poet's eye, in a fine frenzy rolling,*
> *Doth glance from heaven to earth, from earth to heaven;*
> *And, as imagination bodies forth*
> *The forms of things unknown, the poet's pen*
> *Turns them to shapes, and gives to airy nothing*
> *A local habitation and a name.*
>
> –from "Midsummer Night's Dream"—spoken by Theseus, Duke of Athens, to Hippolyta, Queen of the Amazons—by William Shakespeare (1564-1616)

Interesting projects have come my way as part of being Florida's Poet Laureate: judging delightful high school reciters of poetry, for example; or introducing America's Poet Laureate, Juan Felipe Herrera, at the Palladium. A recent and moving opportunity arrived recently when I was asked by a young poet-choreographer, Luis Lopez-Maldonado, to write an introduction to "The Brillantina Project," a collection of 49 poems written in remembrance of the victims at the Pulse nightclub in Orlando, America's worse massacre since 9/11.

In a way, poetry is about names, and naming things. Don't write "flower," I tell my students. Write "amaryllis," "begonia," "dandelion." Instead of "boat" write "sloop," "sailfish," "outrigger." Names have a resonance that is particular and individual and, when writing about people, poetry's aim is to give these names a kind of immortality, preferable than being simply cut in stone—libraries are warmer than graveyards: *We have lived, and our lives had meaning.* So the Project begins with the names and photos of the 49 victims.

On June 12th, 2016—fifteen years after 9/11—a madman entered the Pulse nightclub, the most popular gay bar and dance venue in Orlando, Florida, and shot and killed 49 people, wounding 53. The Brillantina poems are in memory of them, to help us grieve, to celebrate their lives, to recover, and remember.

This wanton slaughter of innocents wasn't, of course, an isolated incident. In America, the Pulse tragedy, though larger, joins the ones that took place in Virginia Tech, Sandy Hook, San Bernardino, Killeen, and elsewhere. America has the longest list, but this isn't just an American or LGBT phenomenon, as the bloody massacres in Paris, Brussels, London, and Nice have shown. Evil has always been with us, but technology—the combination of instant electronic communication and easy access to automatic weapons—has made us see it more graphically than ever before.

The perpetrators tend to be young males, often speaking of some political or religious cause, but in fact they are unhappy, unsuccessful, sexually confused, jealous of those who seem to be satisfied and enjoying their lives. (The murderer at Pulse, divorced and remarried, was, among other things, a wife beater.) Hence, the attacks take place in restaurants, schools, train stations, and nightclubs like Pulse, busy places where people gather to learn, to travel, to have a good time. The damage the killers do is unspeakable, but they cannot win, and the way to defeat them is to continue on our positive paths with even more resolution than before. In "If I Am Murdered" Miguel Morales writes, "Tell them / they didn't kill me—they unleashed me."

"The Brillantina Project" unleashes the 49 victims on the pages of this moving anthology. Besides their names and photos, poem after poem speaks about our belief and love for them, and brings their lives back. As with the loved ones in our own families, this isn't metaphorical; they really still live in us.

Also not metaphorical: the city of Orlando has announced plans to buy Pulse and, after a proper waiting time, convert it into a memorial of the site of America's deadliest mass shooting.

I'll close with a few more lines by Shakespeare, our wisest poet, born long before the idea of an LGBT community had emerged; but who knew what evil was, and that every single human life is a poem.

But thy eternal summer shall not fade,
Nor lose possession of that fair thou owest,.
Nor shall Death brag thou wander'st in his shade,
When in eternal lines to time thou grow'st;
  So long as men can breathe, or eyes can see,
  So long lives this, and this gives life to thee.

–from "Sonnet 18" by William Shakespeare

KIMBALL PIANO

DECEMBER 22. 2016

The Dying Kimball

At Christmas my sisters and I
learned to sing carols in German
Grandpa would give us a quarter
apiece for performing though
only Carol could carry a tune . . .

–from "Stille Nacht, Heilege Nacht" by Peter Meinke

The old piano is dying. Our trusty piano tuner came around last month, as he does every November, and did his usual plinkplunkplonking over the yellowing keys, getting us ready for the traditional holiday music. As he gave us the bill, he said with upfront sorrow, "In all honesty, I think it's not worthwhile for you to pay me for tuning this anymore. Nothing left in there to tighten or splice." It's not one of the smaller makes—spinet, console, or studio—but a dignified Kimball upright, dark brown, weighs a ton. It has an elegant carved frontispiece, and feet that look like chipped classical columns, which makes us think it was made in the late 1880s or 1890s. But we don't know. It arrived at our house unannounced while we weren't home.

In a surprising coincidence, both Jeanne's mother, Ruth, and my mother, Kathleen, were wonderful pianists. Jeanne and I suspect our stubborn "creative gene"—that early itch to draw and write—stemmed directly from them, bless them both. When Ruth was young, she played classical concerts on the radio; and Kathleen gave piano lessons for most of her life. A piano was a natural piece of furniture in our houses as Jeanne and I grew up in our separate towns: Rainbow Lakes, NJ, and Brooklyn, NY.

After we moved into our cottage in Driftwood, I (apparently too often) complained about not having room for a piano. Although my playing skills were never high enough to get me a job in a dank bar, I could read music, and enjoyed picking out folk songs and, around this time, Christmas carols. So, one day Jeanne and I came home from an extended trip, opened our front door—and there loomed this domineering piano, taking over our small living room like a Trojan horse. A short note from our kids said, in essence: *Here it is: deal with it!*

It was crazy idea (and what an effort it must have been for the youngsters!), but we were deeply touched (sometimes we say "doubly" touched, as the children hadn't completely paid for it). Of course we kept it. The piano fortunately was on rollers, and eventually, by taking out a door, we tucked it neatly against the windowed wall in Jeanne's rectangular studio, which consisted of a sturdy table, a file cabinet, a good light, and some built-in bookshelves. And now a large piano.

The studio soon became the second most communal room in the house (the first being the dining room). After dinners we and our guests often crowded around it to sing. This being Florida, our casement windows were usually open, and we could serenade the passersby with "Underneath the Lantern," "Molly Malone," and at Christmas time "O Little Town of Bethlehem" and all the Usual Suspects. Some of our friends were fine singers, soloists, and members of choirs who could make a joyful sound no matter who was playing the piano. We even serenaded Larry, the lizard who lived on the windowsill behind the piano. We couldn't reach behind it to catch him and set him free outside, so Jeanne left saucers of water so he wouldn't starve; occasionally he'd peek out to listen judiciously. He seemed to live, for a lizard, a long and happy life.

We had some gorgeous times around that old piano. Now, with some impairment of my never very flexible hands, combined with its own disabilities, our Kimball mostly sits in stoical silence, except when visiting children give it a poke.

It's still beautiful.

Merry Christmas.

> *Certain melodies can break your heart*
> *just seeing them on the page their plump ovals*
> *bobbing like sea gulls on the surface*
> *of some moonless tide . . .*
>
> –from "Minuet in G" by Peter Meinke (both quoted poems from *Liquid Paper: New & Selected Poems*, Pitt Poetry Series, 1991)

2017

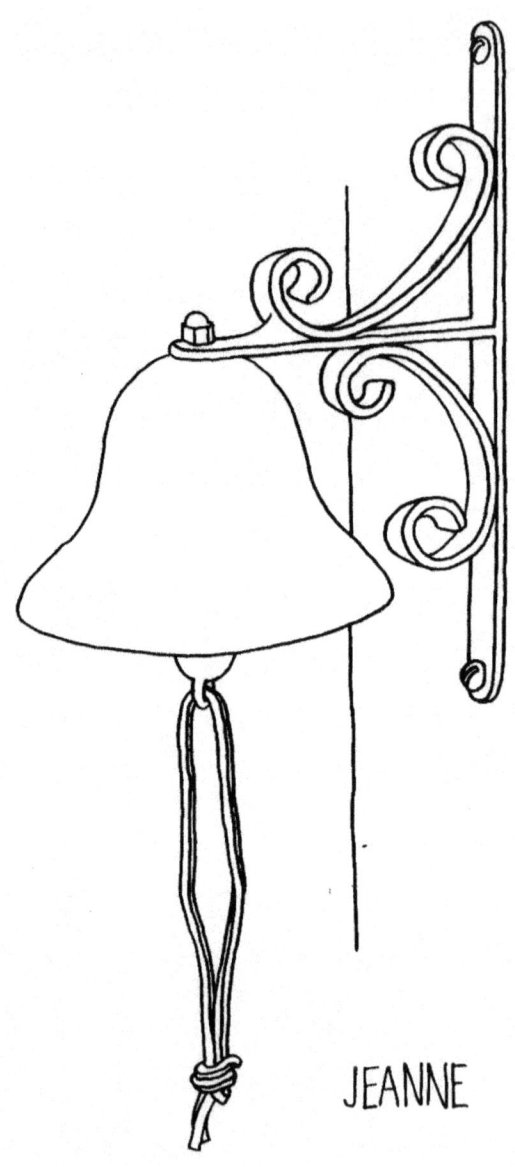

THE BELL

JANUARY 5, 2017

Ringing in the New

Ring out a slowly dying cause,
  And ancient forms of party strife;
  Ring in the nobler modes of life,
With sweeter manners, purer laws . . .

Ring out false pride in place and blood,
  The civic slander and the spite;
  Ring in the love of truth and right,
Ring in the common love of good.

2016 has gone. Let it go. It was the worst year in our memory, at least since 1963 when President Kennedy was assassinated; and Thich Quang Duc, a protesting Vietnamese monk, publicly burnt himself to death, boiling up the Vietnamese War into our national consciousness.

We thought we'd start 2017 in a foul mood, bringing to mind the mordant New Year's Eve wish of the Poles struggling under Communism when we lived in Warsaw; translated to today the toast as the bells rang out would be: "May 2017 be worse than 2018." That was as optimistic as the Poles could get.

But for the last two weeks, we've had a rich, invigorating, and inspiring holiday visit from our farflung children and four grandchildren (Sophie, 11; Julian, 9; Tai, 8; and Kai 6). It was impossible to sit around our overflowing table, looking at these healthy, handsome, intelligent and responsible citizens without being optimistic about

America in spite of everything. (It was also impossible to sit there without spilling a glass.) We want to be responsible, too, so our beautiful grandkids will live long and happy lives, and grow up proud of their country.

So although it's true that from the beginning of 2016, we began calling our president-elect a nut case, we're going to begin this year by letting the grandeur and dignity of his office wash over him, at least for a while. We'll keep our eyes open, naturally, remembering one of a poet's inherited tasks is speaking truth to power. With President Trump, this will become tricky.

Everyone says, for example, that we should take him seriously, but not literally. I've taught English all my life and know that kind of sentence is aimed at giving the person, in this case Trump, a passing grade; but what it means exactly is *Although he's continually lying his gold teeth out, don't worry: in the end it will turn out all right.* Well, OK. He won, didn't he? Because of the office, we shall hold off a bit, but keep our eyes wide open, like his mouth. (We'll still allow room for a little snarkiness.)

President-elect Trump has already chosen a cabinet that looks like it's ready to whisk insurance out from under the ragged shoes of the poor; make further cuts to our struggling public school system; undermine our progress with climate change; and rescind rights from women that have taken a century to achieve. This list could go on— but as they haven't actually done anything yet, we'll wait, and hope somehow they'll behave better than their records indicate.

The Russian novelist and outspoken critic of authority Aleksandr Solzhenitsyn (1918-2008) said in a 2005 interview on Russian television, "Democracy is not worth a brass farthing if it is installed by bayonet." He was talking about our efforts to influence Iraq and other countries, but looking at our recent Russian-flavored election, I'd suggest that democracy isn't worth a tin ruble when installed by fake news, misleading government announcements, blatant lies, and an archaic system. Both candidates played in the same game, of course, like football players in a snowstorm. But in this particular game, Trump was the professional and Clinton the amateur.

No one likes a poor loser, shouting *"The system's rigged."* Let's wish Trump and his gang, and all of us citizens, the best of luck in 2017. And may their luck and our luck coincide.

> *O living will that shall endure*
>   *When all that seems shall suffer shock,*
>   *Rise in the spiritual rock,*
> *Flow through our deeds and make them pure . . .*
>
> *With faith that comes of self-control,*
>   *The truths that never can be proved*
>   *Until we close with all we loved,*
> *And all we flow from, soul in soul.*
>
>   –both quotes from "In Memoriam A.H.H." by Alfred, Lord Tennyson (1809-1892)

Photo by Diane Cohen

PETER AND JEANNE MEINKE

ABOUT THE AUTHOR AND ARTIST

PETER MEINKE, Poet Laureate of Florida, has published over 25 books, with poems appearing in *The New Yorker*, *The Atlantic*, and *Poetry*. His awards include three prizes from the Poetry Society of America, two NEA Fellowships, a Fulbright Professorship to the University of Warsaw, and many others. He has been Distinguished Writer-in-Residence at Davidson College, Emory University, University of Hawaii, Hamilton College, Thurber House, and other schools and organizations. His most recent book is *The Expert Witness* (2016), a collection of short stories. His earlier collection, *The Piano Tuner*, received the Flannery O'Connor Award for Short Fiction. He's read his poetry, fiction, and children's books at schools and universities throughout the United States and at the Library of Congress, as well as abroad in London, Paris, Warsaw, Geneva, Africa, and elsewhere.

JEANNE MEINKE's pen and ink drawings have graced the pages of *The New Yorker* (over a hundred times), *Gourmet, Bon Appetit, Yankee, Early American Life, Gastronomica*, and other magazines. She's also collaborated with her husband on two children's books, most recently *The Elf Poem* (2015), and six poetry chapbooks, including the prize-winning *Campocorto* (1996), plus his book on writing, *The Shape of Poetry*. Their latest book together is Peter's short story collection, *The Expert Witness* (U. of Tampa Press, 2016). Since 2007, Jeanne and her husband have been collaborating on a bi-weekly column called "The Poet's Notebook" for *Creative Loafing*, an alternative newspaper in the Tampa Bay area. A collection of her drawings, *Lines from Wildwood Lane*, was published by the University of Tampa Press in 2010.